Living
with
Teenagers

Cassell Lifeguides

Cassell 'Lifeguides' are books for today's way of life. The increasing trend towards a 'self-help society' is an indication of the need for reliable, helpful information in book form, as less and less advice is offered elsewhere.

With this series, Cassell furthers its reputation as a publisher of useful, practical self-help books and tackles subjects which are very much in line with today's lifestyles and problems. As people become increasingly aware that situations need to be looked at from all sides, they can turn to these books for realistic advice and encouragement.

Setting up Home by Fiona Buchanan
Living with Teenagers by Tom Crabtree
Coping with Separation and Divorce by Jean Stuart
Staying Healthy by Mike and Tricia Whiteside
Ready for School by Maggie Wilson

Living with Teenagers

Tom Crabtree

CASSELL

Cassell Publishers Limited
Artillery House, Artillery Row
London SW1P 1RT

First published 1989

British Library Cataloguing in Publication Data
Crabtree, Tom
   Living with teenagers — (Cassell lifeguides).
   1. Adolescents. Behaviour. Psychological aspects
   I. Title
   305.2'35
ISBN 0-304-31667-9

Typeset by Litho Link Ltd., Welshpool, Powys, Wales.
Printed and bound in Great Britain by
Courier International Ltd, Tiptree, Essex

Contents

Introduction

Place: our house. Time: six years ago. An enormous teenager knocks at our front door. 'Ugh, ugh,' he says to me. On hearing the visitor's voice my son rushes downstairs and plaster falls from the hall ceiling. The two ETs engage in conversation. 'Ugh, ugh,' they say. 'Nah, nah.' Baffled, I retreat to my study.

One morning, also six years ago, I left Dorset for London. My eldest daughter was sitting on the front doorstep, chatting on the telephone to a friend. When I returned at 7 pm she was still there. My God, I thought, the phone bill. Fortunately, it was a different friend. My daughter had lots of friends and used to run a free agony aunt service for them all.

It isn't easy living with teenagers. Your own teenagers may be too talkative, noisy or silent. They may treat the house like a hotel, never tidy their bedrooms, play their transistor radios or music centres when what you want is a bit of peace. They may quarrel with you (or with each other), stay out late, have you worried sick about their speech, behaviour or dress. Teenagers can be appalling.

They can also be great fun. We had three, all of whom have now left home. Two are abroad and one is at university. The house, believe me, is terribly quiet without them. I don't know whether nostalgia casts a golden glow over everything, but I miss them a lot.

That's why I'm writing this book. I want you to be able to offer practical help, plus genuine care and support, to your teenagers. I want you to ask, in return, for some consideration of you as parents and as adults who live in the same house. Living together means give and take *on both sides*.

I'd like you to have some sympathy for them. I mean, would you like to be a teenager again? I wouldn't. I'd like to be 35 again. I'd like to be 40 again – a lovely age, when we have the experience to know what we want, the zest to enjoy it, the sense not to rush it. Teenage? No thank you. It's a time of self-consciousness, awkwardness, of looking in the mirror and never being satisfied with what we see.

I was around when they invented teenagers. They were invented in the 1950s along with rock 'n' roll and Teddy boys (and girls). In 1955 'Rock around the Clock', played by Bill Haley and the Comets, was the number one pop record in Britain. By 1957 teenagers, aided and abetted by Elvis Presley, Buddy Holly, Gene Vincent, Fats Domino, Little Richard and Chuck Berry, had really arrived. They had their own way of dressing, their own slang, their own music. Rebellion was in. Conformity with adults was out.

What we saw in the mid-fifties was the birth of a new word ('teenager') and the emergence of a new high-profile group, most of them at work, most of them with money to spend. From 1945 to 1950, the average teenage wage increased twice as much as the average adult wage. The record industry, together with the magazine industry and the clothing industry, realised that this was a huge market. Why not produce something distinctive for them, something *different*? Teenagers arrived on the scene, and they've been with us ever since.

Of course, there have always been young people. The Greeks and Romans complained about them. 'The ripeness of adolescence', Plutarch wrote, 'is prodigal in pleasures, skittish, and in need of a bridle.' Moliere, the French playwright, wrote in 1661: 'Young people hereabouts, unbridled, now, just want.' Even then, adults had grave reservations about the young. Remember Shakespeare's *A Winter's Tale*? In it, the shepherd says: 'I would there were no age between ten and three and twenty, or that youth would sleep out the rest; for there is nothing in between but getting wenches with child, wronging the ancientry, stealing, fighting.' This sounds remarkably like me in one of my more pessimistic moments as a father of teenage children.

Young people in the past had a much lower profile. They had to grow up quickly. There were 12-year-old able seamen at the Battle of Trafalgar. General Wolfe scaled the Heights of

Quebec when he was 19. Many working-class women were working by the age of 12, married at 16. Youth was a brief interlude between childhood and the responsibilities of the adult world.

Nowadays, we allow youth a moratorium on adulthood which seems to last an eternity. On their 13th birthday they're teenagers, but when are they adult, when do they fly the nest and start looking after themselves? Nobody, these days, starts work at the age of 13; girls don't go into service like their great-grandmothers did; men don't start earning their own living at the age of 14 like my father.

Those young people, teenagers, live at home with us. They have their own tastes in music, dress, conversation. They have their own beliefs, views, ways of seeing the world, construing it so it makes sense to them. How do we learn to live together with them so that we can see each other's point of view?

Let's get back to sympathy. Think what it must be like for a teenager living in today's world. There is unemployment, crime, terrorism and gangsterism. They turn on the television and learn about famine in Africa as the Western world decides what to do with wheat or butter surpluses. They learn that the USA and USSR still can't agree about nuclear arms control.

What are they to make of it all? They must sometimes think that the adults by whom they are surrounded are absolutely barmy, that the world has gone mad and that evil is, slowly but surely, triumphing over good. They go about their lives knowing that hard drugs, alcohol, pornographic films and cigarettes are available to them if they want them. They live in a world which is unsure about its spiritual values and political priorities; a world which seems to be confused, nasty and selfish. No wonder they are confused themselves.

There is also pressure on teenagers from their own peer group. To be really accepted by the group they may have to speak in a certain way, wear distinctive clothes (which are a kind of uniform – a way of signalling togetherness). They may have to adopt certain attitudes to life, follow certain fads (e.g. 'posing'), have their hair done in a certain style.

These pressures are not easy to resist. All teenagers have a desperate need to belong, to be accepted by their peers. Those peer groups are the half-way house between childhood and adulthood. In them, teenagers have to cope with that most difficult of all questions: 'Who am I?'

A friend of mine, a psychologist, almost had a fit when his daughter came home one day with a gold earring through her nostril. Only the week before his son had had his hair dyed pink and cut in Mohican style. 'It's their need to belong,' I told him. 'Yes,' he muttered. He seemed less than convinced that they had to establish their identities *that* way.

The question of identity is crucial. Teenagers are forever looking in the mirror. Like Adrian Mole, they worry themselves sick over their spots and pimples, over whether they are sexually attractive. Girls worry about their breasts (too big? too small?), boys worry about their penises. Both sexes worry about their complexions, their hair, about whether people like them. It's a time of uncertainty about oneself, a time of exploration, a time of trial and error, with identity as well as clothes. Most parents, looking at it, find the whole thing totally exhausting.

What is astonishing, in the face of all the pressures upon them, is how many teenagers there are who care about others, are socially minded, and have a vision of a better world which they hold fast to through thick and thin. There are *some* teenagers who are violent, selfish, brutish. There are many more teenagers who are caring, sensitive and idealistic.

This book is about all teenagers – the good, the bad and the disillusioned, those who hope for a better deal from adults and those who have grown sceptical about the world in which they find themselves. Teenagers are, first and foremost, human beings. If they live with love and courtesy, they will grow up to be loving and courteous. If they live with common sense and consideration for others, they will learn to be sensible and to consider the needs of others. If parents ask nothing from them, that's exactly what they'll get.

That's why I don't think the Them and Us aspect of bringing up teenagers should be overdone. There *is* a generation gap; there's always been a generation gap, and a good thing too. That gap ensures that teenagers (and parents) can have some space to themselves, can do their own thing, live their own lives, make their own mistakes, have a little freedom.

There are two worlds, two circles, but those two circles overlap. Parents and teenagers do have things in common. Each of us is a human being at a particular stage of life's journey. We can teach teenagers courage, optimism and hope. We do that by caring about them, not being afraid of them, saying what we need and want, asking them what they need and want. We have to have sympathy with them and empathy. We have to see things from their point of view.

'Love 'em and leave 'em be,' somebody once said to me about teenagers. That's good advice. Love them, show you care, but give them some responsibility and space to lead their lives. There'll be good times and bad times, there'll be humorous times and times when life is hell. You'll go through patches when you're alienated from or baffled by your own children. Expect that, too.

There'll be unconscious rivalry. As a teenage daughter approaches womanhood (and many teenagers, boys and girls, are astonishingly beautiful), poor old mum may be struggling to keep her figure, worried about her looks, or approaching the 'mid-life crisis' when she knows that she is no longer as young as she was and that she'll never see 30 (or a 22-inch waist) again.

You'll know that feeling if you have a teenage daughter. But what about dad? He sees his son growing taller than he is, perhaps bringing home an incredibly attractive girlfriend. Poor old dad, meanwhile, is just noticing a decline in his physical prowess. He knows he'll never play right-back for Arsenal, he can't return cross shots at tennis as he once could, he can't run and be sure of catching his bus. His hair is growing grey. When he looks in the mirror he sees someone who looks startlingly like Oliver Hardy, and certainly bears little resemblance to Paul Newman.

It *is* a problem. It can lead to jealousy, even the projection of one's frustrations and anger on to an innocent teenager. The main thing is to know that it's happening and to be honest with yourself. I remember the first time my son beat me at tennis. 'I'm growing old,' I said. I wasn't angry, just sorrowful. That's better than shouting at him later for not tidying his bedroom. I did tell him off about his bedroom, but that had nothing to do with the tennis. When I say you have to try hard to be honest, I want you to believe me that it isn't always easy.

What I think is curious in today's world is that parents receive lots of advice and help in bringing up young children. There are mother-and-toddler groups, playgroups, nurseries and plenty of magazines (e.g. *Mother*, *Parent*, *Contact*) giving practical advice on bringing up infants. A parent with a problem can find help and, often, other parents to talk to about his or her troubles.

If you have teenagers, on the other hand, you receive very little help. There are no magazines to help you, far fewer books, no groups you can go along to when you want to talk about the crisis you're facing at home. If your son is a football hooligan, or your daughter has started drinking with her friends in a local pub, whom can you turn to for help?

I think this is strange, because parents know that boredom and aimlessness are vital factors when it comes to teenage vandalism. Yet what *do* you advise your son or daughter to do if he or she happens to be unemployed? What do you say to your teenager if she or he refuses to do homework, or won't help in the house, or goes out with friends who you think are totally unsuitable?

Do you have rules in the home and, if so, how many and about what? This books aims to help parents live with and adjust to teenagers. It deals with boy- and girlfriends, hair-styles, staying out late, discipline, sex, drugs, negotiation and, most important of all, being friends and being honest with your own teenagers. It advocates the middle way, a way of common sense. I don't want you to be Genghis Khan, Sigmund Freud or Florence Nightingale. I just want you to be you, ordinary parents. I want you to have sympathy and common sense.

You know, it was much easier to bring up children 50 years ago. Both my grandmothers had 12 children and they were marvellous women, serene and intelligent, optimistic, kind and gentle. Then, there were ways of doing things. Parents knew their own mind, and children knew that parents had to be obeyed.

Nowadays, it's much trickier. Parents themselves are often tired, confused, worn out. The teenagers are faced with an enormous number of moral and personal choices. They look to their parents for guidance in making those choices. How can we give them that support and guidance when we ourselves are often baffled by this rapidly-changing society in which we live?

The answer is, we must be honest. We must do what we think is right and stick up for our values and say what they are. We mustn't duck out of our role as parents and adults. That's no way to help young people. It merely makes them more vulnerable to adults who don't care about them and who will exploit them.

We care. That means negotiation and honesty. It means building up a relationship with them in which we can be open and give them something of our true selves, give them some of the things they need and also tell them what we want and need. We're entitled. Parents have needs as well as teenagers, so don't be ashamed to stick up for yourself, your values. Permissiveness is just another word for sloth and moral cowardice. Permissiveness, not having any 'no' in your family dictionary, is a cop-out.

A doctor friend of mine told me that, one morning, her teenage children were being particularly argumentative and complaining at the breakfast table. She went into the kitchen, took hold of a large pan of lukewarm porridge, and threw it at them. It had a salutary effect. For months afterwards, if one of the teenagers raised his or her voice at breakfast, the others would say: 'Cool it. Leave it out. Remember the porridge.'

I can't recommend throwing porridge at teenagers, but I can recommend a few rules and the occasional use of that word 'no'. All human groups have to have rules and have to negotiate with each other what those rules are to be. I'm sorry to go on about rules, but no human group can live in harmony without them.

When you negotiate with others, including teenagers, you need a Relationship, Information and Options (RIO). You need to be honest, to know what's happening and to know what choices you have when it comes to solving the problem. In the family, as in the political world, jaw jaw is always better than war war.

When you are negotiating with your teenagers, don't be bossy. Have a sense of humour and don't set out to be perfect. There are no perfect parents, no perfect families. There are only good-enough parents and families who struggle through, sometimes making a total mess of things. If you try to be the perfect parent, you'll end up disappointed, disillusioned and dismayed. Be you, do it your way, *but be consistent and honest.*

Sometimes, you'll make a fool of yourself. I remember one evening hurrying home from work, after a really busy day, and dashing up to the loo. I saw my wife, totally naked, bending over the bath. I smacked her on the bottom.

'Hello, darling,' I said, 'what a lovely bottom you've got.' Then I dashed downstairs again. There was my wife, and the teenagers home from school.

'But who?' I asked.

'That lady in the loo?' said my daughter. 'It's Sheila, a friend of mum's. She's staying the weekend.'

I told my children what had happened. The worst thing of all was that when Sheila came downstairs my wife said to her:

'This is my husband. I don't think you've met.'

We had.

My teenagers thought that was hilarious. They loved me making mistakes. They considered my hair to be really terrible, my record collection (*Carmen Jones*, Nat King Cole and *Selections from Paul Robeson*) extremely *weird*. They thought my clothes antediluvian, my moustache a disaster. I didn't shave my moustache off. I'm me. They're them. We're different and the good things are not all with them. I had no intention of getting a Mohican or buying an electric guitar. I prefer Paul Robeson to Wham!

That's fine. I had no intention of apeing them and I know that they had no intention of wearing corduroy trousers and an old, threadbare pullover. That's my style. They have theirs. What we had together is that we were human beings, in the same family, living in the same house, same road, same world. I wasn't going to force my views of the world upon them, but I wasn't going to let them foist their view of the world upon me. That's not parenting. That's folly.

I remember when my three children, then aged 11, 13 and 15, went to stay with friends. They were told by their hostess: 'Do what you like, when you like.' They did exactly that. They ate when they felt like it, roamed the streets at midnight, watched the late, late films, went to bed at 3 am. Nobody washed dishes, tidied the house or did any other jobs. Surprisingly, after a week of complete freedom they were glad to get back home.

'I didn't like that set-up at all,' said one of them. 'It was chaotic.' They looked tired out, fed up and completely done in. Giving youngsters freedom is a very responsible thing to do. The responsibility lies in giving them freedom they can handle; it doesn't lie in letting them do what they like, when they like. That's not freedom. It's terrifying. For them. For any of us.

I hope what follows will give you a framework, some principles and some rules of thumb for dealing with your own teenagers. Do it in your own style, your own way, but stick to that road called common sense which leads on to an avenue called negotiation. I hope that leads you on to friendship. That's the aim of the whole thing. After living with teenagers it would be great to end up as friends. To move from love to friendship, from the protective love that children need to the warm, honest friendship that we have with those we like a lot.

The thing to do with your teenage children is to spend some time with them while you've still got time. Our house is uncannily quiet without them. No plaster falling from the ceiling, no tremors as the pop music blares out from upstairs, nobody on the front doorstep telephoning friends when I come home in the evening. I miss them.

Somebody once said to me: 'I never liked my teenage children very much. I suppose I never got to know them.'

That's sad. They're worth knowing, worth talking to, worth *listening* to. Teenagers have said to me: 'My best friend is my mum.' Others have said: 'My best friend is my dad.' That's a marvellous thing to say. It is not all roses with teenagers, but it is not all doom and gloom either.

Years ago on television, I saw a young and successful actress being interviewed. She was about 25, extremely beautiful. The interviewer asked her where she went at weekends. Expensive night clubs? Trips to Paris? Out with her boyfriend?

'I go to see my parents,' she said. 'I like them and I like their company.'

Incredible compliment. What a tribute to the parents.

I won't patronise them, those teenagers. Or you, either. This is a tough world we're living in and it's not easy to get things right, but we have to try. I hope what follows helps you to get it better. We're not aiming at perfection. We just want to try to get it right — for them and for us. They are, sometimes despite appearances, human beings, like I said.

1
Laying down limits

Your daughter slams the living-room door and rushes upstairs. Her parting shot is: 'You miserable, neurotic cow, I hate you.' That's because you won't let her go to the disco. It doesn't finish till midnight and she has to be at school the next day. You've put your foot down and been abused for your pains. You feel hurt, angry, humiliated. What happened to the little girl you used to be so close to?

'Why haven't you tidied the house as I asked you?'

Your son gets up from the chair where he's reading *Melody Maker*. 'Oh, shut up,' he says. 'You're always getting on at me – about my hair, my clothes, my friends, everything. I can't do anything right in this awful, bloody place. You make me sick.'

With that, he goes out of the front door. His parting shot is: 'Grow up.' At that moment you wish he'd leave school and find a job, preferably in Outer Mongolia. You have a strong desire to follow him out of the door and throw the shopping at him.

Where have you, as a parent, gone wrong? Is it like this for other parents too? Am I a total failure as a mother or a father? No. You *will* go wrong, have arguments, have moments of despair. It *is* like this for other parents and you're *not* a failure. You're just human, and so are those teenagers. It's not easy to live with people without having differences of opinion, or emotionally upsetting scenes. Arguments are par for the course. It's all part of living together, adapting to other people's needs and wants. It's not an easy business, even in the best-regulated families. In ordinary families, like yours and mine, it sometimes seems impossible to get it right.

Let's look at it, first, from the parents' point of view. You'd like a happy, peaceful home, you've worked hard enough for it. You love your teenagers but you don't want them taking over, imposing their needs on you all of the time. You want a bit of peace, to watch what you want to watch on television, a rest from the noise of transistor radios. You'd like to understand your teenagers more but they seem to resent you opening your mouth and saying what you want. They won't help in the house unless you make a fuss, or tidy their bedrooms, or think about what *you* might like and enjoy. There seems to be a wall between you. You know that adolescence is a difficult time, but is that any reason to be inconsiderate, ill-mannered and self-centred? Why *do* they treat the place like a hotel? Why don't they respect you more. You try very hard and they just take you for granted.

The teenager (and he or she *is* entitled to an opinion) thinks that you *fuss*. You're always going on about things that don't really matter, like the dishes, the state of the kitchen, the shopping, meals. Who cares about all that? You're always prying into my life and you never let me do anything. You won't let me go to the ice-rink and *everybody* goes, you keep asking stupid questions and getting hysterical when I tell you the truth. I'm the only person in this place who's sane, the only one who doesn't fly off the handle about the slightest thing. What are parents for? All they ever do is moan at you.

Two views. Same family. Both parents and teenagers have needs. Parents *will* feel angry from time to time, lose their tempers, run out of patience with a rude or over-taciturn son or with a daughter whose main aim in life seems to be to get out of the house. Parents have needs and rights. So do teenagers. How can we get those needs met without turning the family into an army camp or a chaotic mess where everybody spends their time shouting at each other?

What you need to deal with teenagers is a style of parenting, and what I advocate is an open, robust style. It's based on *negotiation*. For negotiation (rather than domination) you need a relationship, information and options. You need to know that you're entitled to feel angry, fed-up and frustrated. You need to know that teenagers often feel that way, too. You need to know what your limits are and you have to be able to say no when it's necessary. Negotiation is give and take. That's what living together is all about.

This style of parenting isn't one in which you know it all. It's one which involves *listening* to teenagers when they say something. Listening is an important part of any good relationship. Many of us parents can talk; how many of us know how to listen? It involves treating teenagers as sensible human beings and praising them when they've done well. Moaning at them, criticising them, shouldn't be the only two shots in your parental locker. You wouldn't moan at, or criticise, your adult friends like that. What makes you think that kind of approach works with teenagers?

What we're trying to do is steer a middle way between rigid authoritarianism and over-permissiveness. This middle way involves being positive (not coming out with constant 'downers', nagging remarks such as, 'You're not going out looking like that, are you?' Why do you think she's taken three hours to get ready?). It involves having clear limits. (This is to save you going mad.) It involves saying 'no' when you need to. Good negotiation doesn't preclude the use of that useful two-letter word.

Lastly, an effective style of parenting involves giving them PPR (Praise; Prestige; Responsibility). Praise works better than criticism; prestige is vital to all human beings: we all want to count for something. As for responsibility, if we don't trust them, how can we prepare them for the outside world, how can we turn them into self-reliant, *response-able* human beings?

Let's have a look at some of these things more closely. Remember the key word: *negotiation*.

Relationship

You have visitors coming the next day. Your daughter has promised to help you tidy the house and prepare a casserole. She rushes in and says that Sandra, her friend is going to the ice-rink that evening. Can she go with her? You don't want her to go. You want her to stay in and help you. You say:

'You go, darling. I'll manage. I don't mind.'

Good parenting? Kind? Not really. You're left feeling resentful. You mind like hell. You were hoping she'd help you. As she goes out of the door later, you call after her: 'Have a nice time.' She will. You won't. This is the martyred mum situation. You resent her going out (she was the one who wanted the visitors to come). You don't want to do all the work yourself. You're being put upon, and you know it. You're shooting yourself in the foot psychologically. You have a right to express your annoyance but you don't. You could have solved the whole problem by just saying 'no'.

Now let's take scenario two: different mum, different teenager. Your son rushes downstairs and gobbles up his tea, which you have taken an hour to prepare.

'Goen aht wiv Tracey, tonight,' he says. 'Can you lend me a quid?' You feel like throwing the teapot at him. 'Have a nice time,' you say, as he grabs a piece of cheese and rushes out. You feel totally despondent. Doesn't he know you're his mother, not just the cook and skivvy for all of them?

Here's another mother whose resentment and anger is building up inside her. Unexpressed anger is the royal road to depression and it's so silly. We are entitled to express ourselves when we feel taken for granted, put upon, abused. We are allowed to say what we feel, to say: 'Enough is enough.' We are, in a good relationship, allowed to say what we want and need.

These mothers need to know three things:

- *You're entitled to say no.*
  It's those children whose parents never say no who find the world such a difficult place. We should practise saying the word in the mirror and use it from time to time.

- *Lay down your own limits.*
  Don't just sit there stewing with resentment. If you don't say what the limits are, who will? Of course, they'll try to get away with things. Didn't you at their age? It's up to you to say: 'This won't do.' It takes courage, but it saves a great deal of repressed anger.

● *Negotiation isn't letting teenagers do what they like.*
Negotiation involves compromise, trade-offs, give and take. That is what life is about. That, and giving people PPR.

Let's take two examples to see how negotiation and PPR work within a family.

Years ago, my teenagers used to moan at mealtimes ('Not *that* again') and generally behave as though they, having expected The Ritz, were being served up grub which was unappetising, drab and beneath their champagne tastes. 'Boring' was the constant cry. Meanwhile, my wife felt that her efforts were unappreciated. She was becoming a martyred mum. Something had to be done about it.

We had a meeting, discussed it. I suggested that, since there were five of us, we take a day of the working week each. On that day (the Day of Hell) the person responsible had to set and prepare breakfast and clear it away before work or school. In the evening he or she had to cook the evening meal for everyone else and wash the dishes. The food had to be bought the day before each person's D of H. (Money was provided for this, but the person concerned had to do the shopping.)

That stopped the moaning in its tracks. My youngest daughter was 10, but she insisted on doing her day and the meals she served up were simple but good. The two teenagers were more ambitious: they cooked some really brilliant meals. My day was Friday. I sometimes cheated, went out and bought fish and chips. So what? The system worked. It gave the teenagers a share in the responsibility of running the home. It also saved grumbles and moaning about meals in the week (at weekends we did our own thing). Meals ceased to be an opportunity to be nasty to each other. My wife ceased to be a martyr. We all appreciated those days when somebody else was looking after us, doing the work.

Don't moan at your teenagers. Make changes. Alter the way things are done; alter the way the home is run. All young people have to be fitted for survival. They have to be able to look after themselves or other people in an emergency.

When they leave home they may live in a bedsit or flat. What happens, then, if they've never cooked a meal, washed and mended their clothes or changed a fuse? By molly-coddling them in the home, we're doing them no favours. Out there in the big, wide world you can't always call for mum (or grumble at her).

How do you know when to give teenagers responsibility? You have to judge it, look for things they may be able to do and *let them have a go*.

I remember, years ago, my sister-in-law teaching her little boy how to cross the road. She went with him, taught him how to look right and left, when to cross. Then came the time he had to do it by himself. He was six (but mind you, it was only a little road and there was less traffic in those days). She used to watch him, in fear and trepidation, out of the bedroom window. Then, when she knew he'd really got the idea of it, she was able to relax and to leave the responsibility of crossing the road to him.

I tell that story because, whenever you let your youngster do something that's new, different or demands that you lessen your control over them, *you are going to feel anxiety*. That's the price you pay for letting them do things which will help them to mature as human beings. What's the alternative? To keep your daughter as a little girl or your son as a little boy all her or his life? That's not fair. They can only build up confidence by achievement.

Let's take some specific examples of the steady building up of confidence in young people.

Shopping

Let your son or daughter do the shopping. Build up from shopping for the day to shopping for the week. Say: 'We have a couple of friends coming next Thursday. I want you to shop for the meal and cook it.' Let them have a go. It's surprising what they'll come up with if you give them the responsibility. Fix your cost limit and let them decide whether it'll be spaghetti or chicken supreme!

Babysitting

When your son or daughter first starts babysitting, make sure it's a house nearby so you can pop in or telephone just to make sure everything is OK. Then, when you know that they can cope, they can babysit for other people you know, assume the responsibility and earn a bit of extra money. With my own three teenagers this was a major source of income. It was a real responsibility in a real-life situation.

Clothes allowance

As soon as they're 13 or 14, say: 'Here's your monthly allowance. Buy your own clothes.' They will make mistakes (unsuitable shoes, gaudy shirt, awful blouse). So what? They'll learn by taking over the responsibility. If you have doubts, go with them first and, when you think it's OK for them to do the choosing, let them. Why not?

Paper rounds

Make sure you're sticking within the local bye-laws on the employment of children (your local reference library will advise you). This gives a teenager an opportunity to earn money, to save up for something, and to get that newspaper through that door on time!

Organising study

Help them with this at first. Show them how to set out a work programme, how to be systematic in what they are doing. Then, leave the responsibility to them. No nagging. Just say: 'You handle it.' Give them help at crisis times, but leave the major responsibility to them.

Driving

They'll start off in the car watching you drive. When they're legally entitled to drive, get them a provisional licence. Start off in a very quiet road or big, empty car park. Let them have a go. Then, pay for some driving lessons for them. Let them have plenty of practice in driving by you sitting in with them (I did this for all three of mine). When they have good road sense (and a few more driving school lessons), let them take the test. Then, you have to bear the anxiety as they take the car out by themselves. That's part of the price you pay for being a parent, but how else will they grow up if you don't lose your fear of letting go and let them assume responsibility.

The principle is simple. *Give them more responsibility, not less.* I hope you will have started when they're young with some of these, but do make sure that they assume responsibility for their teeth (regular visits to a good dentist mean fewer fillings), their bedrooms, getting in at a certain time. (Negotiate the time. Stick to it. If they let you down, say how angry you are.) What you want is a gradual increase of responsibility, small steps, leading to a gradual increase in confidence.

They may want to go camping. Let them camp in the garden and then, with friends of the same sex, at an approved camp site. Then, a mixed group of them may want to go camping at various camp sites within visiting distance. Let them do it. You have to learn to trust them sometime. If they're into walking and youth hostelling, let them have plenty of practice in simpler walks before they try mountain walking where they'll be responsible for judging the weather and the danger involved. This is the principle of The Duke of Edinburgh Award Scheme. Build up to that time when they can go off by themselves for a week and know how to look after themselves, what to take. They have to take the responsibility.

How can they learn to live their lives if we guide them too much? *Let them handle it.* If your son or daughter wants you to answer the phone and give excuses to his or her friend about something, say: 'No. *You* do it.' If you have a son or daughter who hates tidying up, give him or her a specific job to do (for example the vacuuming) and say: 'Right. You can do the cooking at weekends. I'll do the washing up and your tidying jobs.' *Discuss* awkward issues. Come to agreements about friends, times in, who does what and when.

'That's *your* responsibility' is a vital phrase. Don't keep your youngster a little boy or little girl. Let them tackle things, even if they do fail from time to time. Don't nag, moan or whine at them. Just say: 'You handle it.' In that way you are teaching them to take real responsibility for themselves. That's what they need if they are to make a good adjustment when they leave home and have to face up to the problems out there, outside the family.

Don't keep them as children. That's your need but not theirs, and it's unfair on them. Don't patronise them or treat them as bumbling idiots. That may be your need to be superior, to be in charge. Again, it's not fair on them. They need to let you know what they can do, so why not give them the chance? Perhaps you want your teenagers to stay like children because you feel, underneath, that their growing up means you're growing old. That's understandable, but hard on them: they need to be trusted and given a chance to use their skills and aptitudes.

That Day of Hell wasn't only about giving our teenagers a job to do and responsibility. It was about praise and prestige, too. We were able to say things like: 'X is great at making omelettes, Y is brilliant at salads.' Those are ego-boosting remarks, and all human beings need them. We all need prestige. If we're told we're competent, super people often enough we get to believe it.

Praise was given for cooking and for other things when praise was due. Not lavishly. Just a few words of appreciation. 'That's great.' 'You did marvellously there.' 'Well done.' That's all that's needed. We all need encouragement, we all need praise. After a while criticism ceases to work with me. I just curl up, get bolshy or apathetic. Praise works on me like a charm. If somebody praises me I'll do my best for that person. I know it works that way with me, I'd guess it works that way with you. What makes us think it works any other way with teenagers?

In general, reward works better than punishment. That's why we have to give teenagers praise when they've done something helpful or achieved something they've tried hard to do. Praise is a powerful reward. To notice them only when they've done something wrong, to criticise them when they've disappointed us or made a pig's ear of something is no way to motivate human beings. Be positive.

To deny the child in others, to deny how powerfully that child cries out for praise and words of encouragement, is to deny the child within ourselves. We need it; so do they. When we realise how praise and criticism, forgiveness and blame, appreciation and being taken for granted work *for us*, then we can deal effectively with motivating our teenagers, negotiating with them. When did somebody last criticise or blame you? How did you take it?

Information

Teenagers *are* trying. They *can* get on our nerves. Think of it from their point of view, though. They're trying to be what you want them to be; they're trying to be people who are worth while, valid, autonomous. They're trying to do that in the face of their own doubts, anxieties, confusion, fear, inner struggle. That's why they need limits. They have to know what it is we expect from them, what the boundaries are. It really is frightening to live in a world where you don't know the rules, don't know what's expected of you.

So, have a few rules. Not too many but make sure everybody knows what they are. Give them *information*.

'Can I have new shoes?' says your son.

'No,' you say (it's allowed). 'I'm short of money at the moment. I can't afford it. Ask me again next month.' That's fine. You're saying no and saying why you're saying no. That's open.

You're a single-parent mother. Your teenage son asks you: 'How's it going, mum?'

'You say: 'Fine, just fine.' As a matter of fact it's going hellishly. Your relationship with your boyfriend is falling to bits and you have the phone bill to pay. Why not say: 'Things are bad at the moment, son, but we'll get over them. I'm worried about Arthur, and the phone bill. That's why I'm so quiet.' I think that's a much better answer. It's true. Anyway, he *knows* things aren't going well. He can sense it, so why not give him the information he needs? He can handle it. Teenagers aren't stupid: they're often much more insightful than we think.

This openness of information – about your emotions, your finances, your life-situation – is vital. It's what we don't know, aren't sure about, that scares us. That's why some of those Hitchcock films are so scary: we don't know what's happening, what's going on. Be open with your teenagers and let them know what's going on, inside you and around you. It is, for them, much less frightening that way.

Teenagers, like young children, have an uncanny knack of knowing when something is wrong in the family. They have an emotional radar system that picks up our anger, grief, depression, even when we don't express it. Having picked it up on their emotional screen, it worries them. So why not tell them? That's what robust and open parenting is: giving them the information to know where you are so they can figure out better where they are. If that single mum had told her son the truth, what would have happened? He'd have put his arm around her and said: 'Poor you.' That would have made her feel better. *And him.*

Options

I've said that good negotiation depends upon a relationship, information and options. Let's have a look at some of the options you'll have as a parent. At this stage I want to concentrate not on telling you what you should do but simply to point out, in various situations, what your options are. Let's start off with an example from when my son was a teenager and told me one day at breakfast that he wanted to buy a motorbike. He didn't have the money yet but he was saving up to get enough to buy the bike.

I had several options: say nothing (acquiescence); say, 'Over my dead body;' say, 'I don't like the sound of that' (be scared but do nothing); or say, 'That's fine with me.' There was one more option. I, personally, am really frightened about motorbikes. I keep reading in the newspaper about young people having accidents on them. The last thing I wanted my son to buy was a motorbike.

I said to him: 'I'll tell you what. If you save up for a car instead, I'll help out with driving lessons and give you something towards the car. Whatever you save up, I'll match.' Then I told him that I was really scared of motorbikes and that I'd much prefer him to save up for a car. Was the way I went about it bribery? I don't know. I did know my feelings and I expressed them, as I had a right to. He opted to save up for a car. (When the time came he bought a music centre instead, but that is just one of Life's Unsolved Mysteries.)

Say your daughter, aged 15, asks you if she can go to a party at the house of a friend. 'It's an all-night party,' she adds. You can say yes or no. You say no.

'But Jo used to go to all-night parties when she was my age,' argues your daughter. Jo's her eldest sister, now aged 18. It's not quite true. Jo went to a party like that, you remember, when she was 16. But Jo was very mature for her age, sensible and reliable. Tracey, at 15, isn't.

'I don't think you're mature enough,' you say. 'You can go till midnight and I'll come and collect you. You're certainly not staying all night.' That's an option you're entitled to. It will lead to tears and the accusation that you're not being fair. So what? That's how you feel and you have a right to say 'no'.

Often, we have more options than we think when we're negotiating. We can say yes, instead of no, if they badly want to go to the disco on Saturday night, but we are entitled to insist they catch the 11 pm (or last) bus home. That's a condition of our saying yes. That's negotiation.

We used to let our teenagers have the occasional party in the house. There were two conditions. We'd go out, but we'd come back at midnight and go to bed, so we didn't want to find drunken teenagers all over the house. Any damages had to be paid for. That was the deal. For us, it worked.

It might not for you. You have to lay down your own limits, take up options to suit you. You may not be at all worried about your son or daughter having a motorbike, but you may live in fear for your Ming vases should the local teenagers have a party in your house. Say how you feel, say what you think, listen to what the teenagers have to say and decide on an option that suits you. Each family is different, but the principles of negotiation are always the same.

It's a two-way thing. Tell them your worries. Tell them that you feel awful if you do. Tell them about the mortgage, the rates, the electricity bill, the shopping bills. Get them to do the shopping so they *know*. Stick up for yourself and what you believe in. All teenagers have a need to rebel, but how can they rebel against you if you don't tell them what you stand for, hold dear, think important? They're not always right. We know a thing or two, us old 'uns, us wrinklies. Tell them what your values are. They won't know what to reject and what to hold on to unless you do. Teenagers count. So do parents.

I hope we're getting the hang of things. You lay down the limits to suit you, say what's acceptable and what isn't. Expect them to try it on. That's when you have to make the limits clear, have the courage to say no.

Don't be rigid; try to be fair. Expect some teenage contribution to the family (ask nothing from them and that's what you'll get), but let that contribution be according to age, aptitude and ability. Look out for situations in which you can confer prestige and give praise. Accentuate the positive; leave out the constant nagging.

Be open and honest. Let them know what's going on. Treat them as intelligent human beings and don't forget your sense of humour. Things will go wrong occasionally. You're not perfect and they don't want or need you to be.

Have some rules. You'd be a mug not to. No group can exist together without rules. Just have enough to make the home a reasonably liveable place to be. Amend the rules from time to time if you need to. Say why you have those rules, what they're for. It's tough to insist on the few rules you have, but it's a lot tougher without them.

Don't say thoughtless things like, 'You're useless.' Teenagers are very sensitive. A few thoughtless words can really hurt them. Why not discuss it, or at least say why you're so annoyed. That's common sense. It's also the open style of parenting.

Be robust. Come out with it. Don't hide things from them. If your marriage is going through a really terrible patch, tell them just that. They'll know anyway. If you want them to paint the kitchen ceiling rather than go ice-skating, say so. A few open words are worth weeks of resentment. Don't let the sun set on your wrath. Have it out with them. That's what you'd do with a friend, and teenagers can be friendly and open with us, if we give them a chance.

They want, above all, to know where they are with us, what they can and cannot do. Then they have a definite framework in which to lead their lives, a set of principles to accept or reject. They need that. They have enough problems of their own without us heaping confusion upon them.

2
The teenager's private world

Firstly, physical changes. With the onset of puberty the pituitary gland, the leader of the endocrine orchestra, stimulates the endocrine glands to pour various chemical substances, hormones, into the bloodstream. In girls, the ovaries secrete oestrogen; this leads to development of the breasts and initiates the menstrual cycle. In boys, the testes secrete testosterone which causes growth of the penis and of facial hair.

Boy's shoulders broaden, girls' pelvises become larger and their hips become rounder. Boys have a greater development of muscle and bone. They may have an odd, angular look with their feet, hands and nose large in proportion to the rest of their body. Girls develop a layer of subcutaneous fat which softens the contours of the face and body.

These physical changes have been well-documented elsewhere. What I want to do is to concentrate on the emotional changes which accompany them – the heightened self-consciousness and self-awareness. The changes may be followed by shyness, touchiness, self-doubt, an obsession with looking into the mirror, or rudeness, brashness, noisiness.

'My son carries a transistor radio everywhere with him, like a comfort blanket. Is there anything wrong with him?' one mother said to me. There isn't. He's just a teenager and he's tuning in to the teenage culture that we adults provide for him. An enormous tranny is, too, a very good way of staying in your own world, cutting out the voice of parents.

What we have to remember in considering the private world of teenagers and the generation gap is that teenagers *are* different from us: they're younger, fitter, more exuberant, they have more hope. We also make them different. We collude in the generation gap and supply, as adults, many of the artifacts of their culture: videos, pop records, clothes and (criminally and tragically) drugs. We adults also emphasise the Us and Them. We say we want them to act in a mature way, but we don't treat them as though they were intelligent human beings. Often, we're jealous of their youth, envious of their freedom. We send them confusing signals. We, as parents, resent their high profile and, sometimes, even their presence. We say we care about them, but I think we're slightly afraid of them. Many of us refuse to listen to them. We put them down, patronise them and, often, confound their hopes.

Let's take a simple idea: listening to teenagers. Years ago I saw a 13-year-old boy in the clinic. His father had died when he was an infant. He then lived in his grandfather's house, with his mother. A year previously his mother had been killed in a car accident. Then his grandfather died. The lad hadn't spoken since. What we did in the clinic was play chess. On our first meeting I'd said to him: 'You can speak if you want, but only if you want to.' He didn't. Winter changed to spring and the games went on, in silence.

One morning, in April, he looked up at me and said, 'Your move.' He started speaking after that. I think what he wanted to know, before he could trust himself to speak, was that I was really listening and had some idea, however tenuous, of what it was like to be in his shoes.

If I were a teenager today, I'd be slightly sceptical, if not downright angry, about the facile assumptions that adults make about young people. The word 'teenager' is a label we stick on. Then we assume that most of them are punks, mods, rockers, glue-sniffers or football hooligans. Teenagers get a bad press, and this confirms our worst fears about them. We hear about them when things go wrong: we don't hear much about the thousands and thousands of socially-minded, sensible teenagers getting on with their lives, trying to make some sense of this anxiety-stricken, crazy world.

We exaggerate the differences between teenagers and ourselves. Certainly, teenagers do ask themselves questions such as: 'Who am I? Do people like me? What am I good at? If people knew what I was really like, would they still like me?' Sensitive adults ask themselves those questions too. Adults make mistakes, make a fool of themselves. Adults worry about their appearance, weight, their attractiveness-rating and about unemployment, nuclear war, the state of the world. We don't say of adults that they're like that because of their hormones. We'd say, of adults, that some things would make anybody worry.

Perhaps adults don't worry about masturbating. If they masturbate, they know it does them no physical harm and that they're entitled to sexual fantasies (and to explore their own bodies). Adults do, however, worry about sex, about the size of their penises (or breasts), about their relationships with the opposite sex. Teenagers haven't cornered the market on this sort of thing. Mostly, adults aren't open and honest about all this with young people. This widens the generation gap.

'It's her hormones,' we say of a daughter who is difficult to live with, who appears to be selfish, inconsiderate and noisy. It isn't. It's just that living with anybody in close proximity for any length of time is difficult. People have conflicting needs. They need privacy, and some degree of contact, closeness. It isn't easy for adults living together to get the formula right. What makes us think that it will be any easier living with teenagers?

False expectations, false assumptions: that they, teenagers, are all the same (a 13-year-old is very different from an 18-year-old); that all teenagers are in a constant state of emotional turmoil, identity crises, obsession with their boy- or girlfriends or their spots. We generalise too much about them, give them money instead of real humanity and understanding. We patronise them. We give them a junk-food diet of heroes from the pop world rather than encourage them to identify with adults who are worth something, who can enhance their self-esteem. We don't tell them the truth, we don't tell them about life as it is. Life is tough. Why don't we tell them the truth about it, rather than expose them to a pop culture in which the rewards go to the performers (mostly non-teenagers) rather than to those who are in the audience?

Let's get back to listening. I asked six teenagers what worried them most in their lives. I've read *Catcher in the Rye* (J. D. Salinger, Penguin books) and *The Secret Diary of Adrian Mole, aged 13¾* (Sue Townsend, Methuen paperbacks), and I thought perhaps that the teenagers would go on about adults being 'phonies' or maybe, like Adrian M, reveal their secret worries about spots on the chin, their girl- or boyfriends, GCSEs, sex, masturbation, love. They didn't talk about these at all (perhaps that's because they were talking to me). Here are their answers to the question 'What worries you most?'

Mark, aged 16

'My parents. They split up last year. They'd been throwing furniture at each other for a couple of years, arguing like kids. I was glad when my dad left. I hope he's OK, but I doubt it. I can't see him surviving on his own without us to boss about. I still like him, I think, though it's better without him here. I worry about my mum. She's great. I hope she's happy. She deserves to be. Adults are weird, aren't they? They're like children really . . .' Mark is six feet tall and has a pleasant, friendly manner. To me, he seems incredibly mature for his age.

After a long pause, Mark says. 'Have you ever thought about adults? You know, really thought about them? I have this theory that because nobody believes in God any more, you know, so there's no heaven so when you die you just go six-foot under, nobody wants to grow old, everybody wants to be young. I think my parents didn't like being parents, they didn't like being adults, they were trying to be like me and my brother' (Mark's brother is 18). 'Does that make sense to you? Mum and dad are a pair of teenagers really, except when they acted like seven-year-olds. You know?'

I do know. It's very sad when parents refuse to grow up, abnegate their role as parents. There's no greater obscenity, to the young, than a 40-year-old pretending that he or she is 20. It never happened in my grandfather's day. Perhaps he had high hopes of heaven. Perhaps he knew that when you become a man or a woman and a parent you have to act in an adult, responsible way. What about Mark? With some teenagers it's a privilege to talk to them.

Gail, aged 18

'My parents. I was sent to a little private school when I was five. I think they wanted me to be a doctor or something. They never asked me what I wanted to be. They live in a beautiful house, real *Ideal Home* stuff. I hate them. I ran away from home at 17 and I've been living in digs since. I live off social security, sure, but that's better than being like them. I hate them and I worry about it. Nobody should hate people that much. The thing I hate about them most is their smugness. They're so satisfied with themselves it sickens me. All they're really interested in is money.' Gail's hair is pink. She is wearing a leather jacket and trousers and has a gold ring through her nostril. She is one of those teenagers who have never been consulted about their needs and wishes, their likes and dislikes, their hopes and aspirations. There has never been any dialogue, any negotiation, any 'What do you think?' or 'Tell me how you feel about that.' When domination replaces negotiation, what you get is rebellion and hate. This is as true of the family as it is of nations.

Frank, aged 18

'Getting a job. I've been on a training scheme for six months now, but I'd really like to get a proper job. Unemployment's really bad around here. I'm always short of money. My dad says I should sell my motorbike, but what does he know about anything? Have you noticed the price of bus fares lately?' Frank is engaged to be married. His father lost his job earlier in the year. His mother is the only person in the family who has a 'real' job.

I've said that this is a rapidly-changing and confusing world we live in. Unemployment is one aspect of that world.

In the face of the problems presented to young people who are unemployed, we have no choice but to be absolutely honest with them and to do everything we can to provide jobs for them. A job gives a person an interest, social contact, an identity, self-respect and hope. Young people desperately need and are entitled to all of these.

Laura, aged 14

'The bomb. I mean, we're going to get blown up one day, aren't we? That's unfair, because those old people who take the decisions have had their lives. We haven't. I think they're all mad. Don't you think they look a bit mad? They must be to have things like nuclear bombs in the world. Are you in CND?' Laura is dressed in her school uniform.

Laura, with her abundant charm and her obvious intelligence, reminds me of Mark. I left her with a question in my own mind. Just who are the adults in this world and who are the children?

Clare, aged 13

'My piano lessons. I hate my piano teacher. She's too strict. Sometimes I pretend I've been to the lessons when I haven't. I just walk about. I keep the money. My parents will kill me when they find out . . .'

Not all teenagers' worries are cosmic. Some are quite specific. What's needed is an atmosphere in the home where worries can be mentioned, discussed. Teenagers need privacy. They also need to feel that they can come out with a problem if they want to.

Let's be careful about this. Many teenagers don't want their every move discussed: there are some things they just don't want to talk about. Parents vary in their ability to afford help when needed without seeming to be prying, nosey, overprotective. Perhaps we need more teenage counsellors, in youth clubs and schools, where teenagers can talk to a neutral, objective person about their problems, major or minor. Perhaps we need more P of T (Parents of Teenagers) groups where parents can talk to each other. I don't know what happened to Clare about her piano lessons, but I do know that many teenagers come to harm because they feel that there's nobody they can talk to about their problems. We, as parents, may not have the skill or knowledge to help them; collectively, we should ensure that teenagers know where they *can* get help. Clare won't, she feels she can't, talk to her parents about her problem. Who is there to advise her? I'll return to this important question of counselling and information later in the book.

Jonathan, aged 15

'School. I hate that place, and especially the maths teacher. He goes too quick. If you don't understand anything he thinks you're stupid. It's just that he's a bloody awful teacher. I'm hoping to go into the army and I think you have to have maths for that. Every time I have a maths lesson I feel sick. Somebody ought to report him. He's a fascist pig . . .'

There's something wrong here. One of the biggest factors in a youngster's success at school is parental involvement and encouragement and the link between home and school. Here the link has been broken. A visit from the parents might solve Jonathan's problem. It certainly needs to be discussed. His hatred for maths and the maths teacher is generalising out towards a hate for school. That's a pity, since there's nothing here that couldn't be sorted out by an honest discussion between Jonathan, his parents and the school. When the teenager's home and school never meet, it's the teenager who's left in the wilderness in between.

Teenagers do worry. They worry about big things and small things, but don't we all? They worry about masturbation, so tell them the facts. Tell them that you masturbated when you were a teenager, that 93 per cent of men and 62 per cent of women have masturbated at some time in their lives. Don't make a big deal of it. Just tell them. It's not the words you use but your attitude that counts. That attitude has to be down-to-earth, matter of fact, brisk (and, sometimes, laced with a dash of humour).

If they ask you about sex, be honest. Tell them how inept (and slightly guilty) you felt about it at their age. Tell them what you feel about bringing an unwanted child into the world, tell them where they can get contraceptives if they need them (that is, if they intend to sleep with someone), and tell them about sexually transmitted diseases. Tell them about love, and about how much better sex is if you love someone.

Attitude is all. If you are authoritarian, or by being too perfect yourself make them feel guilty, then they'll reject you and your advice. If you're open and honest, they'll know they can talk to you about their skin, weight problem, sex, or any other subject. A child who's being bullied at school lives in a world which is sheer hell. What makes it hell is not the bullying, it's having nobody to talk to about it. It's not the problem which is crucial for teenagers, it's isolation which does the damage – the feeling that your parents are looking but not listening, telling you what to do rather than saying, 'Tell me about it if you want to.' We have a lot in common with our teenagers, so why don't we share it with them rather than put them down and demand respect from them without earning that respect?

I've said, or rather a teenager has said, that some adults act like children rather than like adults. I think we ought to think about this. It gives us the clue as to how we ought to react to the teenagers around us. What are adults? They are people who have learned to accept themselves and their own limitations, who can look at themselves with a sense of humour and who know that the world and relationships aren't perfect. Real adults aren't worried sick about their face, arms, legs (they know that other people are much too worried about their own face, arms, legs to even notice). Adults are honest with others and honest about themselves. All adults have learned that the greatest happiness in life comes from helping others, not from being obsessed with self.

Human beings aren't butterflies: they don't suddenly emerge as absolutely perfect. Human beings have self-awareness. Human beings are always in the process of becoming. The road towards maturity is a long one, and adults and teenagers are merely at different stages along that road. We adults can't say to teenagers: 'We know everything and you know nothing.' They know plenty. Considering the world they live in, some of them are incredibly sensible and mature. Why widen the generation gap? They need it (they need their privacy, their own space), but they also need our humanity, our honesty, our willingness to trust them, our concern.

Teenagers *will* worry – and with reason. I open the paper today. There's been another hijacked plane, yet another horrific murder, no progress in nuclear arms limitation between the USA and USSR, no progress in South Africa, another massacre of one group of people by another of an opposing creed. Crazy world. Every time I open the newspaper I read of some appalling incident somewhere in the world.

Perhaps the maladjusted teenager these days is the one who *doesn't* worry. Teenagers certainly have plenty to worry about. You, as a parent, have to treat teenagers as intelligent human beings, but be there when they need you to be, and be honest when they need you to be. To deal most effectively with their worries, remember:

- *You can't solve all their problems.*
  You can get help yourself, or tell them where to get help, from various organisations and advice centres (see the list of addresses at the end of the book).

- *Don't adhere to the hormonal theory of teenage.*
  Acquiring six GCSEs or being without a job involves real stress. That's where sympathy and practical support are useful. If you say 'She's worried about her complexion,' you may be totally wrong. Instead of having theories about your teenagers, why not ask them?

- *Give them the facts.*
  If you don't know, say so. (You could then suggest where they could find out.) If they ask you if you believe in God and you're not sure you do, say so. Most of the time

they're not worried about how clever you are. It's whether you're honest that concerns them.

- *Listen.*
  If you're always too busy to listen, always on the go, they'll learn that it's pointless talking to you. That's sad. You'd learn a great deal from them.

- *Keep the channels of communication open.*
  If you've had a blazing row, say something like, 'Phew. That was a bit heavy last night, wasn't it? Sorry about that.' Leave it at that. No more is needed. All human beings who live together argue from time to time. It's better to communicate and argue than not to communicate at all.

- *Tell them what worries you.*
  It's what they don't know that frightens them. Besides, if you're open and honest about your worries, you're encouraging them to treat you as a human being and to be open and honest about theirs.

- *Expect some alienation, some insistence on privacy.*
  They won't let you into their private world completely. Why should they? They're different. They're young. They will let you into more of their world if you aren't jealous of them, or patronising with them. To grow up, they need to belong to the family and to rebel against it. That's tricky. So expect them to do things differently from you, some of the time.

- *Keep out of their private world when they insist on it.*
  Never read their diaries or letters, or rootle through their belongings. You have to learn to trust them. You can't keep an eye on them 24 hours a day.

- *Have chats with them.*
  In the kitchen whilst you're cooking; whilst you're shopping; over a cup of coffee; when you're doing the washing. Chat about hair-styles, clothes, anything. You have to talk about the day-to-day things first if you want them to tell you their more secret fears. Why should they

talk to you about a serious problem if you never trouble to talk to them about what's happening around you?

- *Say, often, 'Tell me about it.'*
  Then let them talk. They'll begin to believe that there *are* adults who listen to them. You could be one of those adults. You could be a listening parent.

The teenage pop culture is meant to exclude adults. It has its own hit records, its own music, its own style. That's fine. However, when we believe that teenagers are totally different from the rest of us, that isn't fine at all. We can share a great deal of the world. We can lessen the generation gap. We must, to do that, learn to like teenagers, to think of them as individuals and respect them. Let them have a private world if they wish, but make sure that they know that the door to your world is marked 'open'.

3
The parents' private world

Two years ago I was giving a talk about teenagers and I mentioned, as a joke, Super-Grot parents, those who never do anything right, whose homes are always in chaos, who are constantly arguing with or dominated by their own teenagers.

When the talk was over, a lady approached me.

'Thank you,' she said. 'I didn't know there were more of us. We ought to form a club for Super-Grots.'

I didn't mean it like that. I wanted to emphasise that there are times in every family when parents doubt whether they're any good at the job they're supposed to be doing.

That's OK. Most parents go through a Bad Patch with their children. Some get it late; some get it early; there are very few parents who don't get it at all. There are plenty of books, written by experts on children, to help parents. The trouble is, the child may not have read the book. You're doing your best. Your child is behaving despicably and you ask yourself; 'Where did I go wrong?'

The notion of the ideal family haunts us. We think we ought to be perfect parents, get it right every time. That's impossible. What we have to do is bear in mind that when things get really tough between us and our children, that's a chance to think, to get to know each other better, to re-negotiate, to clear the air. Arguments can be painful, but they can also get things sorted out. In a family, every crisis is an opportunity to learn something, every failure a chance to do better next time.

You have to remember two things as a parent: we're aiming to be good enough, not perfect; and we will get things wrong from time to time and we have to be big enough to admit it.

We're not brilliant parents, but we're good enough. We do

our best. That's good enough. The idea of the 'good enough' mum comes from Dr D.W. Winnicot and is expounded in his book *Playing and Reality* (Penguin). Winnicot tells us that the 'good enough' mother is one who makes an active adaptation to the infant's needs, starting off with complete devotion and then adapting less and less to the wishes of the infant as time goes on.

This is what Freud called moving from the Pleasure Principle (i.e. having your own way all the time) to the Reality Principle (i.e. having to take into account the wishes, needs and opinions of others). It's what I call loving hell out of them when they're infants and gradually making them more responsible and self-reliant as they grow older. No parent can supply all a child's needs. That's why we have toddler groups and playgroups. No parent can supply all a teenager's needs. Often, a new club joined or a new interest taken up will do more for a teenager's morale than endless discussions with parents as to why he or she is so unhappy. We can do lots of things for them. One thing we can do is to encourage them to do lots of things for themselves.

Think about it. You can suffer with them, sympathise with them, go through hell with them, but you can't pass their exams for them. When they rush, ashen-faced, up the stairs to their books (after a hasty tea), you feel for them and know the state of anxiety they're in. What can you do? What you can do is offer practical help. You can't however solve their problems for them. All you can do is to create an atmosphere in which they have a better chance to solve their own problems.

Take homework. Why not discuss anxiety (and panic!) with them? Tell them that we need anxiety to get us moving. Without a certain amount of anxiety we'd never get up in the morning. To get things done we need to press the panic button occasionally. That's OK. Anxiety about homework is normal enough. The worst thing of all is to sit there and not do it but just worry about it: it doesn't help anxiety and it doesn't achieve anything.

Go to the school and see your teenager's teacher if the homework set is too hard or is causing the child chronic worry and stress. Find out what the school is hoping to achieve from it, and take advice on the best way for your teenager to set about doing the homework.

Get into a routine for doing homework. Make sure that your teenager has somewhere quiet to work away from the TV and the family hustle and bustle. Make sure you have some time when the family is together and can talk about things other than school. Impose a time limit on watching TV. Encourage your teenager to have some outside interests so that school and homework don't dominate his or her life. Where school and parents liaise on homework, there's less strain on the teenager. You can't do the homework for him or her, but you can show a bit of sympathy and take practical steps to make sure your teenager knows that he or she has some family support.

Parents have worries themselves. Both or one of them may be unemployed, or under stress in his or her job. Father may be feeling stale, washed out, may feel that his job isn't leading anywhere, that he's on a plateau or in a depression in his life. His hair is receding, his waistline is increasing, he can't run for a bus without puffing and panting. Some men, it's said, go through a mid-life crisis, or the male menopause. He may start chasing younger women, or dressing himself in jeans and trainers in a desperate effort to look young. He may feel that he's reached a T-junction in his life, that he needs a change, that life isn't leading anywhere. He looks in the mirror and sees the signs of age. His face is beginning to crinkle, if not crumple. His son can beat him at tennis. He knows he's middle-aged and isn't going to make that senior job. He too, may be asking those vital questions: 'Who am I? What is life all about?'

What about mum? Wherever she is, either side of the 40 mark, life certainly isn't getting easier. Teenagers are expensive to keep and they can be demanding. 'Can you give me a lift to the disco?' 'What should I do about this?' Teenagers may be noisy, selfish at times, quarrelsome. Mum may be holding down a job to support or supply the family income. She always has demands on her if she is. She has to do her work and then come in and be a mum. That can be exhausting. The question uppermost in her mind, in the middle of the unceasing demands and strains of family life, may be, 'What about me?'

She may still be an attractive woman, a viable human being, but it doesn't escape her notice that her daughter and her daughter's friends all seem to have 22 inch waists, that they look pretty without resorting to make-up or moisture cream, that her daughter is growing into a woman, a sexual being, and that boys and, sometimes older men flirt with her. When mum looks in the mirror she, too, sees signs of mortality: wrinkles, the odd grey hair, lines on her neck, a tiredness about the eyes. Just when she wants maximum support and encouragement at this T-junction in her life (Do I grow depressed, old, tired, or fight back and make sure I stay a person with wants and needs of my own rather than just a mum?), her teenagers seem to make more and more demands upon her. They want emotional and practical support, but what about her?

There's no easy answer to this. Everybody in the family has needs and wants; that's where humanity (and unselfishness) come in. If one member of the family is going through a crisis, that person may need a lot of support for a certain time. That's OK, providing that one person isn't grabbing all the attention all of the time (or using the house as a hotel in which people have to dash about servicing one person's needs). A family is a shared enterprise, and everybody should contribute.

This includes fathers. Dads are just as important as mums. Some fathers are authoritarian, distant, bossy, strangers to their own children. They see their role in the family as supplying money and little else. They leave the running of the family to their wives. Their attitude to teenagers is that they have nothing in common and the sooner the teenager earns a wage-packet (or, preferably, leaves home and becomes totally independent) the better.

That's sad. Fathers are important in a family. They can be great to have around, good friends, an additional source of emotional and practical support to the mother and to the teenagers. They can be good mates, good fun, people to turn to when you're in trouble, people who listen to you, do things with you, help you make decisions and give you encouragement.

What do fathers do in a family? They're not there just to be a money box, or mend the car, fix the roof and do the garden. Fathers are, or should be, an emotional and human resource. A boy needs a satisfactory father to identify with if he is to grow up into a rounded, well-balanced adult. The father's personality, his attitude to life, his ability to relate to his son in an honest, open way, will form the basis of the boy's notion of authority (and what masculinity and being a man are all about). If a boy can identify with his father (or some of his traits), it solves a lot of his problems. He has a suitable role model, someone to emulate. If he can't identify with his father, he has to look elsewhere, and he may find difficulty in relating to other male authority figures in his life.

A girl, too, needs a father-figure. She learns through her father something of the world of men: how they talk, what they look like, smell like. Her father is her first model of masculinity. Her relationship with him may affect her relationships with men when she's older. If her father is distant or uncaring or bossy she may be suspicious of men. A daughter–father relationship can be very close and reward-ing. 'My dad's great,' more than one teenage girl has said to me. 'I can talk to him. He's my friend.' That's marvellous. It is a gap in a teenage girl's life when her relationship with her father is cold, argumentative and hostile, or non-existent.

Single-parent mothers may worry about their teenagers not having a father-figure in the home. They shouldn't worry too much. It's better to have no father than to have a non-participatory or brutal father. There are plenty of father-figures at youth clubs, sports organisations and various associations which teenagers can join. You could argue that it's better to come into contact with older, caring male adults outside the home than have a totally ineffective (or downright destructive) father-figure inside the home. Ginger-bread, a national organisation that deals with the problems of single parents, is given in the list of addresses at the back of the book.

What you should know as a parent is that these days it isn't easy for any of us to hold a family together. I remember that 15 years ago I was shocked when a headmaster told me that one in 10 of his pupils came from one-parent families. This year it's one in four. We're told that one in three of all marriages in Britain are destined to end in divorce. Since 1971, when the new Divorce Act came into force, the divorce rate has doubled. Britain, together with Denmark, now has the highest divorce rate in Europe. Hidden behind the statistics is a great deal of personal confusion and suffering.

Parents worry about this as well as teenagers. We all have relatives or close friends who have been through a divorce. Teenagers know plenty of families where the parents have divorced or separated. You could say that so many teenagers live in one-parent families that the stigma has gone and the suffering associated with marriage break-up has disappeared. I don't believe this. In nearly all cases of divorce there is some financial hardship and some emotional conflict. Sometimes, the conflict, stress and bitterness involved take a toll of the teenager's self-image and their view of adults. Is it surprising?

What can we as parents do about this emotional battlefield in which we live? We try not to be one of the casualties, one of those statistics, but few of us can completely avoid emotional tension in the home, arguments, rows, resentment, stress and strife. What we can do is to remember what I've said before: *it's the things we don't know that harm us*, whether we're children, teenagers or adults. So we have to tell our teenagers what's going on, so that at least they know there's a reason for what they may otherwise find incomprehensible and frightening.

A father once said to me, 'My wife and I have terrible rows. We both have quick tempers and flare up very easily.' To reassure him, I told him that most couples argue once a week. Some couples argue once a day. You don't, if you do tend to argue as parents, need to quote psychological studies to your children to prove how common it is. What you have to do is show that adults can row and make up, can show affection as well as anger. You have to say that just because you row it doesn't mean you don't care about each other.

Violence in families is surprisingly common. In the United States a quarter of all couples, according to one survey, accept violence as a fact of life and hit each other at least once a year. Physical abuse is very common in marriages in Britain also. Couples argue over money, over sexual unfaithfulness (real or imagined), over in-laws, the children, roles in the home (who does what), lack of participation by one parent in the home. They argue over what to watch on TV, over untidiness, over people's personal habits. Some families argue all the time, and the youngsters in those families vary in their reactions to it all: some are very upset, others accept the war-torn atmosphere of the home as a fact of life.

What parents need to know is:

- *You can't bring up youngsters in perfect peace and harmony.*
  Life isn't like that. Don't feel too guilty about rows but, when they're over, mention to your teenagers that the rows are nothing to do with them and that you still like them.

- *Bring up problems before they loom too large in your mind.*
  Say what your grouses and moans are, if they concern all the family. That's better than quietly stewing with resentment, then one day going berserk.

- *Try to postpone really nasty rows until your teenagers are out of the way.*
  They'll know you've been rowing, but at least they'll have been spared the indignity of rows and the knock-down details of the quarrel.

- *Give each other a break sometime.*
  Get a part-time job, do voluntary work, join a club or an evening class. People weren't meant to be under each other's feet 24 hours a day. Use the family as a safe base from which to lead your life, not as the Battle of the Somme.

- *If your marriage is really in trouble, act like adults and get help.*
  Go to a marriage guidance counsellor. Not all marriages

can be saved, but some can. It's not fair to expect your teenage children to sort out your problems for you.

There should be more counselling groups for parents of teenage children so that the parents can talk about those aspects of family life which they find difficult. For most parents it's the first time they've met these problems, and often they find it hard to cope. The teenagers don't find it easy either. Teenage is a time of firsts: first love, first important exams, first job, first time away from home and, for some, first marriage. It's hard to expect teenagers to cope with all this when parents are having emotional problems themselves. It's hard for parents to cope with teenagers when they (the parents) feel as though they could do with some good treatment, some love and attention, themselves.

I was talking to a woman in a theatre bar. We were talking about teenagers.

'How did you feel when your daughter first learned to drive and went out in the car by herself after passing her test?' The woman said she was terrified. She also elaborated on the fear she felt when her daughter first stayed out late, when she had her first date, when she took her exams, when she went abroad for the first time.

'To live with a teenager is to learn to know a lot about terror,' she said.

I thought that was honest. I used to have those feelings myself. However, this fear is *your* problem not theirs. You must learn to live with it and control it, otherwise you will end up through your need to protect them, controlling your teenagers and not letting them live and learn for themselves.

You can't tell them how to lead their lives or what to believe in. You can try to get on with leading your life and say what you believe in. You can search out a source of help in the community if your teenager runs into a serious problem, and not try to deal with it yourself. You can give up any notion that you're going to be a perfect parent. With teenagers there aren't any; there are only parents who do their best, hang in there, keep the doors of communication open and cross their fingers that their teenagers will find a way through the complexities of the modern world.

Let's get down to brass tacks. Let's answer some of those questions I've posed about problem behaviour. What counts, more than anything else, is your *attitude*. If you're bossy, a tyrant, they'll rebel and reject you. If you never say anything real, never stick up for your needs and wants, they'll think you're a fool and rebel against you and reject you. Before we turn to specific problems, here are a few general principles worth remembering if you are the parent of a teenager:

- *You'll fail.*
  We all do. Bringing up teenagers is like golf. You just try to get to the 18th as best you can. Play it straight down the middle and don't be too fancy.

- *Your teenagers will thrive on encouragement and praise rather than nagging.*
  So will you. Get out of the house, live your life. Don't expect all your rewards to come from the family. No output without input, so make sure you get some social input yourself.

- *Treat them like grown ups, as you'd like to be treated yourself.*
  You then have a right to be treated as a human being yourself.

- *Expect to feel anxiety, fear, even terror, when they try something new.*
  It's par for the course, part of parenting. So is anger, feeling fed-up, and feeling a little envious of them from time to time.

- *Don't look for problems.*
  Tell your teenagers what you expect from them, what it is you want them to do. If you don't they'll spend years waiting for you to say what it is you want (or don't want). Then you'll get problems. They may even create problems just to get some response from you, just to see if you're capable of saying 'no'.

- *Continue to grow yourself as a human being.*
  Your teenagers, as they grow older, don't want to see you fading into a non-person. They want a separate, autonomous adult to relate to, someone who is a person in his or her own right, and a friend. They don't want you living your life through them. That's unfair. It gives them too much responsibility for you.

- *Don't worry about being thought conventional or old-fashioned.*
  Teenagers would rather know where they are than have over-permissive, 'swinging' parents. Stick to what you think is right, don't be influenced by current fashion. There's only one thing worse than suffocating repression by parents. It's parents who haven't got the guts to say 'Not bloody likely.'

- *Talk to your teenagers.*
  It's surprising what you can learn from them. You worry about them, but not half as much as they worry about you. Don't believe me? Ask them.

- *Expect conflict.*
  You may need, as parents, to be needed. They need to grow to independence, to need you less. This can be painful for parents. To give what you have to give – all that love and generosity – and find that they don't seem to need you any more is not easy to accept, but that's what parenting is about. You're the bow, they're the arrows and, believe me, they'll stretch you at times, as we'll learn in the following pages.

4

A home life that works

Let's take a simple model of parenting. Years ago a farm labourer, say, could say to his sons: 'Be like me.' They would follow in his footsteps, talk like him, work hard like him, bring home a wage-packet each week, just like him. A daughter would become, in her turn, like mother. She would learn the role of being a mother and know it was her destiny to have children and rear a family, be a mum. That's what women did.

Today, young people may want to do many things entirely different from their parents. If father has a dull, repetitive job (or no job at all), a son will not want to follow him into that. Father may be part of a once-great but now dying industry; the son will see no future in being like dad. Young women may put having a career as top priority (with having a family something to be slotted in to that career path). Things have changed. We parents cannot act as models for our children and say, 'Be like me.' We cannot offer them a detailed blueprint for living because we simply don't know what the future will be.

So what can we do? We can realise that they will identify with us to some extent. They'll use, take into themselves, those bits of our character they find useful. They'll watch us and see how we go about things and, if our style of going about things works, they'll use what elements from our behaviour are useful to them. We can't solve their problems for them, we can only give them an *attitude* to life, a lifestyle, a way of going about things.

That way should, in my view, be based on common sense, courage and negotiation. It should be a middle way: the way that lies between autocracy and anything goes. If you act like

Genghis Khan, it doesn't help them: in the world outside you have to negotiate with people, so what practice are you giving them in living with others if you're bossy and autocratic? Similarly with anything goes. There's no model for living there, either. An exaggerated egalitarianism provides no real moral or emotional support to a young person trying to cope with the modern world.

So, be open and honest, put your cards on the table. Your teenagers want to know what you think, what you want, what you believe in. Leave them to reject or accept your beliefs (that's their right). Make some demands (that's your right), but don't come across like Attila the Hun. Don't be an autocrat, but don't duck out of your role as a parent either. If you do that you'll find they'll make *more* demands on you (in an effort to find out who it is you are and just what it is you do believe in). Don't let them rule the roost. That house you live in is your home, not a hotel, and you'll only solve your problems of living together by openness and negotiation.

Having said all this, let's look at some perennial issues that crop up between parent and teenager and see how we go about sorting them out. Some of these problems will weary you, tire you out. However, problems, small or large, are never solved by running away from them, so let's start with a few minor problems (which can, nevertheless, cause a lot of argument and make you wonder what happened to your previously happy home).

Tidiness

Everybody has a different tolerance level for tidiness. Some people live in houses that resemble Steptoe's yard, others live in veritable palaces: not a spot of dust anywhere. That's fine. No problem. The problem arises when people in the same family have markedly different attitudes as to what's tidy. ('My husband's so tidy, and I'm not,' more than one wife has said to me.)

Your daughter's bedroom may seem fairly tidy to her. To you it may be strikingly reminiscent of the Black Hole of

Calcutta, or the municipal rubbish tip. Don't bother to nag her. Nagging doesn't work. If your teenagers are untidy there are four things you can do:

- *Have a weekly blitz in which everybody takes part.*
  Give them specific jobs to do. If necessary have a list of jobs on the kitchen wall where everybody can see them. Change the jobs around so that it's fair. Set a weekly time for the blitz. Why should you do it yourself?

- *Encourage your teenagers to invite friends round.*
  This worked like a charm on my own teenagers. Instead of sitting there watching TV (and saying things like 'This place is a hell hole'), they dash about busily tidying up before their friends come. The blitz technique works better, though: that way, adults and teenagers can ensure that friends can come most times without thinking they've strayed on to the film set of *They Died with Their Boots On.*

- *Give them a say in the decor of their bedrooms.*
  If you can afford it, give them the money for paint (and posters) and let them do the decorating themselves. Why not? Give a hand if they ask you. Consult them when you decorate the rest of the house and let them help. The home is a place where you all have to live. Setting a suitable standard of tidiness, a pleasant atmosphere in which to live, is a joint enterprise.

- *Say 'This place is a mess' and then ask 'What are we going to do about it?'*
  Don't do it yourself. Start when they're young and make them responsible as well as you. If you do it yourself they'll make a mess, just to annoy you.

Politics, they say, is the art of compromise. So let's see how this notion of compromise helps us to solve three more thorny problems with teenagers: noise, parties and staying out late.

Noise

I suppose one answer to teenage noise, and to pop music or taped rock bands played at an ear-shattering level, is to buy ear plugs (or, as one couple I read about did, move to a separate house in another town). Another approach is to say: 'There has to be a limit.' Say when your teenagers are allowed to have their music centres or transistor radios on. Buy them headphones so that they can listen without you having to listen as well. Have a few rules as to when it's OK to have friends in and listen to music together. That stereo equipment and record collection mean a lot to them. It's part of their culture. The music which may sound awful to you is part of the teenage tribal dance.

All right, but you can't have rock bands or the latest hits blaring out of your top window at midnight. The neighbours may not like it.

Solutions vary. You can't buy them and all their friends headphones. You can insist they play their records at certain times, for example Saturday afternoons or in the evening before 10 pm. I've known parents who have converted garages, sound-proofed bedrooms and even bought garden huts to deal with this noise problem. Most of us can't do this (we may not have a garage or garden, or be able to afford to sound-proof their room or ours). What we have to do is compromise: give them definite times when they can play their records, and buy them a Sony Walkman for those times when they feel they must listen to the latest hit and we feel that what we want above all else in the world is a bit of peace and quiet.

Yet again, it's the gap between their romanticism and cosmic yearnings and nasty reality (NR). One of the elements of NR may be that Mrs Jones next door is not particularly keen on heavy metal music, especially when played at midnight. She, like you, may prefer Spanish classical guitar music and before 10 pm. That's fine; Mrs Jones has a right to live too. So you must make it clear, right from the start, that they can't make a noise, play their music, when and where they like. They can when you (and Mrs Jones) can stand it.

They can at certain times (that's fair), and they should keep it below 98 decibels or, as you should explain, your eardrums start to explode. Talk it out, come to the best solution you can, but I strongly advise headphones: they are the best solution of all.

Parties

This, again, depends on what your limits are. My wife and I used to allow teenage parties. We'd go out till midnight; return. The two golden oldies would say hello to a few of the guests, then go to bed. In the morning we'd survey the scene. Any broken glasses or crockery had to be paid for, and any other damage. My teenagers had some good parties, and the only problem my wife and I had was what the hell to do till midnight. By the time we got home we were usually so tired out we slept through the noise of the party and let the teenagers get on with it.

Just a minute (you say). I need my sleep, eight hours of it. There are the neighbours to consider. We have a valuable collection of Wedgwood pottery in the living-room. I'm terrified they'll ruin the furniture and smash up the house. That's all right. Say no. Your son asks you, 'Can we have a party here next Saturday?' You say: 'No.' It's your privilege to do just that.

It's no big deal. Parties are something to which you say yes or no, and if you say yes lay down the ground rules. You may be a very relaxed, laid back parent. You may say: 'Have the house for the weekend. Your mother and I will go away.' I wouldn't do that, even if all the teenagers were over eighteen. I'd take the view that it's our house, our property, and I'd like to know what was going to happen to it before I gave *carte blanche* to use the premises for any purpose teenagers liked. Maybe that proves I'm a rigid personality. Maybe it proves that I don't trust them. That's fine. I just value my home too much to lend it out to strangers without me being somewhere around.

On the other hand, you could take a line which is positive and lays down some limits at the same time. Say, 'You can have a party, but on certain conditions.' The conditions you lay down are your own. No more than a particular number of guests. No alcohol (if your teenagers are very young). No drugs. The host or hostess to be responsible for the behaviour of guests. If your teenagers are young, you may want to be there, or back at 11 pm. I can only say that if you do say yes to parties, negotiate beforehand what the rules are, what kind of party it is, and make sure the rules are adhered to. That way you will feel happier about further parties. That way you make them responsible (and more careful whom they invite). If you can't bear the thought of teenagers dancing in your living-room, upsetting your neighbours or lolling about your settee, just say no. That's better than saying yes and then having a big argument about the party the next day. On the next day, make sure they wash up and tidy the house. It was their party, not yours.

My own children's parties finished when they wanted them to finish. There were no drugs. They were older teenagers so there was alcohol. I trusted them enough to leave it to them not to disgrace themselves. They had a good time. I'm glad the parties took place, despite my wife and me waiting, like Cinderella, for midnight so that we could go home again. You'll have to make up your own mind on parties but, whatever your decision, give your reasons or your conditions.

Staying out late

Say what you want. For young teenagers you'll want to know where they are, what time the last bus is, whether they expect you to pick them up in the car, what time they expect to be home. If they are babysitting and the people are late back, perhaps they could phone you. Similarly, if they miss the bus, they should be able to ring you and make sure you know what's happened. The time you want them to be back home is up to you. They'll argue for the latest possible time. To insist on a given time, depending on age and sense of responsibility, shows you care. On the other hand, you have to give them some responsibility for themselves, some trust. That's where compromise comes in.

Don't make an issue of it. Tell them what time you'd like them to be in. Explain that when they're late, or you're not sure what time they're coming back, you get really anxious and can't get to sleep, and start worrying about them. 'Do you think 11 pm is fair?' you could say to a 14-year-old. If he doesn't, let him tell you why. Listen. Then, bearing in mind the logistics of transport, find a time suitable to you both.

If your teenager is older and stays out one night till 2 am, and you feel anxious and angry about it, say what you feel. If you say nothing you'll get resentful and negative. Say, quietly and without quarrelling, how you feel and what you want done. Your teenager could: stay out late but come in quietly so as not to wake you up; come in earlier because you don't sleep anyway until he or she is in bed; phone you at, say, 10.30 pm to let you know everything is OK and say what time he or she will be back. Arguments, flare-ups, anger and fear about young people staying out late solve nothing. A sensible discussion is better. If your teenager gets upset that he or she has to be home by midnight, stick your ground. If he or she says that his or her friends can stay out till they like, stick your ground. Sometimes with teenagers you have to put your foot down (quietly but firmly). It shows you care. Look at those bus timetables together, know who's giving them a lift, how they're to get home. Then trust them. If they want to get up to mischief they don't have to stay out late to do it.

Modesty

Common sense works wonders with teenagers. I was recently asked by a mother what to do about a 13-year-old girl, very well developed, who wandered about the house in her pants and bra.

'Tell her she has a wonderful figure,' I said.

As soon as the mother said this to her daughter, the semi-clad wanderings ceased. Neither of us is sure why. Perhaps the daughter just wanted to know that somebody had noticed her recently-emerged womanhood and to receive praise and reassurance about it.

Another mother of a girl (also 13) was very worried that she had seen her daughter masturbating in the bathroom.

'Have you said anything about it yet?' I asked. She hadn't; she didn't know what to say. 'Just tell her, *à propos de rien*, that lots of teenage girls masturbate, that you used to masturbate when you were her age, or (if you didn't) that every girl is curious about the sensations she can evoke from her own body. What's so wicked about it? That's the message you want to put across. It takes away the guilt and the shame. It takes away the compulsion to masturbate out of anxiety and fear. It leaves the daughter (or son, if it's a parent talking to a son) free to choose whether to masturbate or not, and to do it because it's OK to want that pleasure and want to explore bodily sensations.

Compare the effects of being told 'That's wicked' and 'It's no big deal. Most people do it' on a sensitive teenager. One approach makes them isolated, lonely and afraid. The common sense approach makes them feel that they're quite normal, and that feeling, believe me, is very important to teenagers.

Privacy

The same principle (common sense) applies to privacy. I should think that, since Adrian Mole's observations have become public property, half the teenagers in the land now keep secret diaries. Teenagers need some privacy. It enables them to feel they have a life of their own, an area which is their own territory marked by a sign, KEEP OUT.

Should you keep out? I think you should. It shows respect, it shows you appreciate their need to be independent, free of constant vigilance. If you pry too much (go into their room, see what's in the drawers of their dressing-tables or wardrobes, or even worse, read their private diary or letters), what do you achieve? It proves you don't trust them. It means they'll learn to be more secretive. It means that they'll deeply resent this intrusion into their private lives. You wouldn't do that kind of thing to a good friend, so why should you do it to them?

Old habits die hard. Maybe you went into their bedrooms before they were teenagers to look for something, tidy things up, sort out just what happened to those new PE shorts you bought him or her. Things are different now. That means that they have to learn to be responsible for themselves. You won't achieve closeness by prying; all you'll achieve is a brick wall, cemented with anger and resentment. You won't make them response-able. You will lose their respect and esteem.

Money

One way of tackling teenagers responsibility is through the handling of money. You could give them a fixed amount, depending on the age of the teenager and your income but saying, 'If you want more money you'll have to earn it yourself.' The teenager could take a paper round, a holiday job, do gardening jobs, cleaning cars, babysitting, helping in a shop, or even be paid for doing certain jobs at home such as wallpapering a room or retiling the bathroom.

The positive side of this is that it makes the teenager realise that money is hard to come by: it doesn't grow on trees. Being paid for doing jobs in the home, however, involves the risk that a teenager may feel that he or she ought to be paid for anything that he or she does in the house. You have to be careful that the co-operative, helpful attitude isn't changed into one in which the teenager says, 'I'll do it. How much do I get paid for it?'

One advantage of earning money (as opposed to being given pocket money) is that it does give the teenager some independence: he or she appreciates the value of money more and can spend it on what he or she likes. If you've had a part-time job to pay for your own transistor radio or music centre, it's a good feeling to know that you bought it yourself by your own efforts.

Some parents give their teenagers a weekly or monthly allowance out of which the teenager has to find money for clothes, bus fares, make-up, LPs and all the other things that a teenager needs. This is good practice for adult life, and means that the teenager has to learn about budgets, about balancing outgoings against income. It encourages thrift and, like having a part-time job, a real appreciation of money.

If at all possible, I think teenagers should supplement their pocket money by part-time jobs and by trying to earn money of their own. Not only does it encourage independence, it makes them realise how hard parents have to work for their money, and it releases teenagers from the indignity of having to beg for money when they want to do something special or buy something they badly want. Money equals power. To always give handouts is to keep our power over them. To say to them, 'How can you earn that?' is to give them power: an opportunity for initiative and a chance to learn something of the harsh economic realities of the world. Nothing is worse than spoiling a teenager by giving him or her money on demand and then letting that teenager go out into the real world. If your teenager asks for more money and you can't afford it, say just that. Then explain why you can't afford it. That teaches them something about money. If you want more of it, it's your problem and you have to use your own initiative and energy to solve it.

Perhaps I'm giving the impression that dealing with teenagers is easy. It isn't. They can be hypersensitive, stubborn, rude. They can be very difficult to cope with. You have to know what choices you have, the best way to deal with a situation (honest comment? a bit of psychology?), and you have to be aware of their feelings as well as your own.

It's always better to talk to teenagers rather than lecture them, better to listen to them rather than harangue them. Try to reflect back their feelings, the emotions that they're going through as they're talking to you. 'I can see you're angry,' you can say. 'That must have upset you.' 'You must have been absolutely furious.' 'How embarrassing. You must have felt terrible.' This is listening to the space between the words, listening to what they're really saying. That's empathy: seeing it and feeling it from their point of view.

What is also important with teenagers is to know when to play it cool and when to speak out openly and honestly (and show your anger if you feel anger). You should, in general, save the putting your foot down approach for big issues. If you make a scene out of every issue, every difference of opinion, you will perhaps run out of credibility and conviction when it comes to really vital matters.

Swearing

Swearing is an instance of what I think is a fairly minor matter (but annoying), and one which can be dealt with by simple psychology rather than by a rigid, over-reactive approach. Swearing either bothers you or it doesn't. In some houses everybody swears. I find swearing rather boring, so when one of my teenagers started to swear I used what is known (at least to me) as the Iron Filings Rule: when you go north, they (teenagers) go south. If we wear our hair long, they'll wear it short; if we dress smartly, they'll look like tramps who've just scrambled up a railway embankment; if we eat steak, they'll become vegetarians. Just to be different.

What I did was to start swearing at meal-times and every other time I opened my mouth. My wife started swearing too. This more picturesque speech had a remarkable effect on all three teenagers. They all started to speak like Mary Poppins – no swear words at all. I noticed, too, that since I'd grown my hair long my son went out and immediately had his hair cut short. Teenagers, believe me, don't always want to be the same as us. They need to be different; they need to find a place in the car park of the family where they know they have some space and that space isn't occupied by parents.

Sometimes it's difficult to know whether to use an open, honest approach ('Anybody who takes drugs is a fool. Just say no;' more on this in Chapter 6) or whether to use psychology. It depends on the situation, how strongly you feel about it, and what the consequences of your approach are likely to be.

Unsuitable friends

If a particular friend of your teenager bothers you, you can say, 'I don't like him' (or her). That's honest. You can say, 'I wish you wouldn't go around with X.' That's honest. I don't think you can say, 'I forbid you to see X.' How would you enforce that edict? How would you ensure that there were no meetings you didn't know about? You're entitled to your opinion. (Although your teenager might say 'You don't know him' (or her).)

Another way of handling it might be to make it clear that your son or daughter can bring any friends home. Many friends are transitional, they come and go. If we forbid a particular friend to come to the house it gives that friend an added allure, the attraction of forbidden fruit. Why not let the friend come round, talk to him or her and not prejudge? Even if you dislike the young person intensely, you achieve nothing by rejecting him or her out of hand or forbidding your teenager to see that person again.

If you suspect the young person takes drugs, or smokes, or drinks heavily, it's a good chance not to attack his or her character but simply to talk to and discuss with your teenager these tremendously important issues. Say something nice about the unsuitable friend and then say what it is about his or her habits or behaviour that concerns you. Say it quietly and calmly. It's your attitude that counts. What they want from you is an honest comment: a serious and two-way discussion of what's at issue. If you say 'I can't stand X,' it's not good psychology. In this instance it may make them more attracted to X, just to be different.

The telephone

Using the phone is a rich source of contention in many families. It was in my family when my children were teenagers. I paid the bills. I used to tell them to play the game, that phone calls cost money, but judging from the bills I think they used to ring their friends in Patagonia while I was out. What can you do about this sort of thing?

You can have constant quarrels about it, as we used to. You could obtain a pay-phone. (You keep the money they put in the box to make the call. The snag is that the rental is much higher than for a normal phone.) You could change your phone to one that takes incoming calls only. (The trouble with this is that when *you* want to make a call, you have to go out to the telephone kiosk as well as them.) You can have a phone book in which everybody in the house jots down every call they make. (If you stick to this you'll know who's phoning where, and when. This takes trust, however: you can't monitor what phone calls they're making when you're not there.)

This is a tricky one. They seem to need to phone their friends constantly: another day, another *douleur*, or something or other to be arranged. You have to discuss it quietly and seriously and, if there is no co-operation, then get an incoming calls only phone. It's a radical and maybe harsh thing to do, but it does save years of arguments, anger and resentment. In the big, wide world teenagers don't have parents constantly moaning at them. That's the good news. The bad news is that they can't make free telephone calls. Aim for some sort of limit on calls, and if you can't enforce it either put up with the squabbles or buy a different type of telephone. As a parent, and the one who pays the bills, the choice is yours.

Food

Let's take the question of junk food. Your teenage son or daughter seems to eat nothing else, rushes in at meal-times, gobbles up the food you offer and dashes off to his or her friend's house saying, 'I'll buy a Junko and a can of Toothrot on the way.' What can you do about it? In my experience, a long lecture about the importance of nourishing food doesn't work. Neither does having a big argument about it.

What you *can* do is have good, nourishing meals at home and educate their palates so that they know which foods are nourishing and energy-supplying. Let them (as in the Day of Hell) do some cooking, prepare some meals themselves. Discuss diet and food. Let them be adventurous and try cooking a meal they haven't cooked before. If they have non-junk food at home (and do some cooking themselves), they'll learn about healthy food in a practical, common sense way.

They may still eat junk food, but at least they'll know it's junk.

Have proper meal-times. Food is a symbol of love. No mother or father likes to cook a meal and have teenagers arriving late at the table, dashing off before the meal is finished, or getting up to have a long telephone conversation in the middle of a meal. Sit down together. Talk. If anybody rings in the middle of the meal, ask them to ring back later. Try to have a meal together every evening. If everybody is busy and you can't do this, have a meal together when you can in the week or at weekends and let the teenager prepare and serve a meal. Then he or she learns that food is an offering and it's very upsetting to prepare food and have people eat it like the Keystone Cops then dash away, taking all that thought and preparation for granted.

Turn this issue on its head. Give your teenagers some responsibility for meals. Then they'll stop whingeing about the fact that the potatoes aren't quite cooked enough, the cabbage is lukewarm, the curry's too hot. It's only when they have had a go themselves that they realise a lot of work goes into the preparation of food. More important, they're given an opportunity to show initiative and love by being the cook and not always the guest. It's a good preparation for adult life; it saves a great deal of nasty arguments over meals eaten as though an earthquake was expected imminently.

In all these areas, however, trust is vital with teenagers. It's built up by talking to them over the kitchen sink about sex, about contraception, about drugs ('Just say no' – then say why), about smoking, about their friends. Talk whilst you're out shopping, or cleaning the house. Keep it natural and honest. Tell them about when you were a teenager, about friends of yours that your parents didn't like, about your boy- or girlfriends, about sexual attitudes in those days, about the mess you made of some of your dates. Have a sense of humour. Come over as a human being. Be open about your life and let them know that you trust them.

Trust and friendship beat bans and sanctions all ends up. If they want to let you down and see an unsuitable friend, smoke, take drugs, indulge in casual sex, they will. The best card you have to play is to be human, friendly, open and honest and let them know that you *like* them. Teenagers have lots of difficult choices to make. Our job is to offer honest comment and respect for them. There's no way we can force them to make the right choices when it comes to friends or money or anything else. We make ourselves vulnerable so that they can be strong, and we trust them and hope that they'll behave sensibly. It's all we can do. We can't live their lives for them, no matter how much we try to protect them from danger.

Remember to treat your teenagers differently, according to their place in the family and their own personal strengths and weaknesses. Your job is to build them up, to encourage, rather than to put them down. You will have rows, quarrels, scenes. All families squabble. So what? The main thing is to come out with self-respect on both sides. You do that by negotiation, not domination. You do that by quiet explanation rather than by saying, 'Because I said so.' That may work with five-year-olds; it demeans the teenager and is no help to them in resolving squabbles in later life.

Say your 16-year-old son starts to wear make-up. You could say: 'I don't think much of that,' or 'I'd rather you didn't wear make-up.' If he's determined to wear make-up (and especially when you're not around), he will. Using the Iron Filings Rule, you'd be better off saying: 'That looks nice, dear.' (He'll probably stop wearing it the next day if *you* like it.) Or you can simply say nothing. Ignore it. What you mustn't do is shout and scream about it. 'Can I borrow your eyeliner?' puts it all in perspective. 'You look ridiculous' gets his back up, makes the issue more important than it is, and makes him more determined than ever to wear even more colourful make-up, just to shock you.

If your 15-year-old asks if she can go camping with a group of friends including boys, and you think she's not sensible enough to know how to handle the situation, you can't tell her that. What you can say is: 'No. I don't think that's a good idea.' She'll argue, maybe say something like 'Sharon went camping when she was my age.' That's true. Sharon is her older sister, but she at 15 was very sensible, mature for her age and you could trust her. That's fine. Teenagers are different, and one may be given responsibility at a certain age while another may not be ready for it.

So you say: 'I'm sorry darling, you can't go.' Then explain that you'd worry if she went camping in a mixed group; that you don't like the idea of it and you feel that she isn't ready yet to be given that kind of freedom. Sharon, you could say, was exceptionally grown-up for her age, but she's not. 'You feel disappointed and angry,' you could add. 'I know that. But you're not going because I don't think it's wise.' That's the end of it. Make sure that you give your daughter some kind of treat that she can handle (and that Sharon didn't have). That makes it fair. Giving in to emotional blackmail doesn't. There are times when you simply have to say no.

You can't say to your daughter, 'You're more easily led than your sister was,' or 'You're less mature than your sister.' Both remarks are put-downs, hurtful. You can say the situation is different now. It's a more dangerous world, there are more temptations. You can redirect her by saying, 'You can't do that,' (say it firmly) 'but if you show me you're acting responsibly over your friendships, I'll consider it again next year.' Then, give her a chance, some responsibility, to prove she can act in a mature way. You haven't put her down, and you've left the channels of communication open.

Imagine three teenagers at breakfast. One wants scrambled eggs, one a boiled egg, one a poached egg. If we have time we give them what they want (or let them cook what suits them). It's the same with personality. No two people are the same, no two teenagers are the same. We should try to give them what they need, according to age and ability. The aim is always the same, however: to make each one more responsible for him- or herself and to make the most use of his or her talents.

Some teenagers appear self-contained and don't seem to need as much love as a brother or sister. They *do* need love: they just like it expressed through a quick word or a little, inexpensive present. They get embarrassed if you try to show them too much overt affection. Some teenagers are punctual, tidy and responsible. Others are slovenly, always late for school (and always losing letters from school which they're supposed to bring home).

If you have a teenager who likes overt affection, show it. If you have a teenager who's always in a lather about getting to school on time, buy him or her an alarm clock and say: 'As from next week you're responsible for getting yourself there on time.' (If necessary, tell the teacher this is what you aim to do.) Why should you take the responsibility. If you have an untidy teenager and you're tidy, say: 'You'll have to do something about this.' Make sure he or she does. If you're untidy yourself, say: 'We're going to have to do something about this.' Then do it.

Problems arise with teenage children when one is not as clever or attractive as another. You may find that you pay more attention to one child rather than another or that you like one teenager more than another. This happens. What you have to do is not compare too much but treat each teenager for what he or she has to offer.

If two teenagers go to the same secondary school, one may be compared unfavourably with another. ('Why aren't you more like your sister?') That's unfair. The sister may be taller, better-looking, cleverer. So what? The job of the parent (and the teacher) is to find out what the less-favoured child is good at. It is gardening? Cooking? Sport? It's our job to find out, to encourage that interest and develop it.

I once saw two teenage sisters. One was very pretty, top of her class and captain of the school hockey XI. The other didn't seem to be good at anything. She liked art, so I saw the art teacher and we agreed that the girl should be given little jobs of responsibility in the art room and encouraged in her own work in the subject. That teenage girl is now an adult and a professional artist. She became *very* good at art. Everybody's good at something. We have to give them a chance to find out what it is and not say daft things like, 'Why aren't you like your sister?' The answer to that is obvious.

A teenage boy I once saw was, he said, 'hopeless' at school. The only thing he was interested in was cars. Between the school and myself we developed that interest, even found him an old car he could take to pieces (the school made a car pit). That's practical. I saw that boy (now 24) not long ago. He's a car mechanic and well on his way to buying his own garage. We encouraged his talents. That's what we must do with every teenager.

You have a teenager who is good at academic work and aims to go to university. You have another who wants nothing else but to work with horses. That's fine. What are their personalities like? How can you help each one to develop his or her personality? Perhaps one will be more sensitive than the other, need more praise, need a special job in the family that gives him or her a chance to prove what he or she is good at. Being cleverer doesn't equal being better.

You may be surprised to find out that your 'less-bright' teenager is a wizard at computer programming, or is exceptionally good at cooking or hairdressing, weaving, knitting, making greetings cards or mending cycles or motorbikes. I can't tell you what your teenager is good at. If he or she isn't good at school work, do encourage your teenager to find some pursuit in which he or she can express a talent. I've known more than one teenager who failed at school, went on to college (where the work was less academic, more practical) and did incredibly well.

We have to look for that special interest. Art? Swimming? Playing a musical instrument? Woodwork? We have to encourage every teenager to develop his or her own talents. To make disparaging comparisons is very destructive. I wouldn't like it if somebody compared me unfavourably with Shakespeare, or Torvil and Dean. I want to get a little praise for what I do well, and be encouraged in that. Every teenager feels the same way, so we have to keep our eyes open, know what opportunities there are for them to develop a special skill, and encourage them. It isn't a competition. Each one of them is different.

If your son asks you for a new pair of shoes and says that his older brother had a new pair last month, you can say, 'You can't have a pair this month. Last month I could afford it. This month I can't. When I can again I'll tell you.' That's the fact of the matter, so why not say so? You can't treat all your children the same; they're different people. Circumstances alter, you may be going through a hard time financially. Explain the circumstances and try to be *fair*, but don't try to treat your children as equals. They're not. Each has a unique personality, his or her own weaknesses and strengths, and you have to be aware of these when you're talking to your offspring.

My three children were very different from one another – in interests, personality, even looks. What you have to do is to like each one for what he or she is, and encourage their strong points. You shouldn't try to love or treat your teenagers in the same way. Each one should be liked and loved for himself or herself. Don't say, 'Joan never did this,' or 'I wish you were more like Terry.' Comparisons are odious. Every youngster is unique.

There'll be times when you go off a teenager, when you argue, quarrel, perhaps feel you don't like that teenager very much. That's normal. Many's the mother who has told me that her best friend is her son, but that there was a time when he was a teenager when he went through a phase of being totally nauseating. Many's the mum or dad who has a very close and rewarding relationship with a grown-up daughter who has told me, 'There were times when she was a teenager when she got right up my nose.' Give each of your teenagers a special place in your heart and expect to fall out occasionally. After all, that's what we do with our friends, and with teenagers the aim of the exercise is to move from love and dependence to love and friendship and independence, respecting each one's uniqueness as a human being.

That respect has to come through when you're talking to teenagers. It's very irritating not to get a straight answer to a straight question. (*Teenager:* 'What's for tea?' *Parent:* 'All in God's good time.') Some parents talk in aphorisms ('Every day'll be Sunday by and by'), or proverbs ('Don't cross your bridges till you come to them'), or clichés ('Rome wasn't built in a day'). It's more than annoying to be told, when you've just split up from your boy- or girlfriend and are really hurt about it, 'Everything happens for the best.' It doesn't. What about being run down by a number 72 bus?

Reflect back their feelings. Give a straight answer to a

straight question. 'I've just split up from Mark,' your daughter says. 'You must feel bad,' you say. 'Tell me about it.' Your son's looking for his shirt. He asks, 'Seen my shirt?' You answer, 'The trouble with you is . . .' It's not the time for a lecture. Some teenagers have to put up with a lot of this sort of armchair philosophising. 'What time is it?' is answered by 'Where's the watch I bought you? You don't look after your belongings . . .' Quite a few teenagers say that they can't talk to their parents. It's the lack of specificity (or sympathy) that annoys them.

'I didn't get the job,' your son tells you. Don't say, 'I knew you shouldn't have worn that jacket.' Just say, 'I'm sorry. You must feel very hurt about it. Tell me what happened.' Your daughter says, ' I can't remember the number of my combination lock and my bike's chained to the lamp-post outside the supermarket.' Forget Rome, her losing her head if it wasn't screwed on, just say to her, 'Let's think what we can do about this.' Then think, together. Is the number written down anywhere? Do you have to cut the chain? Can you lift the bike over the lamp-post if you take the front wheel off? It's your attitude to her predicament that counts. It's not a good time, whilst she's distraught and upset, to give her a lecture about forgetfulness.

Lectures ('When I was your age . . .' 'The teenagers of today . . .' 'You're heading for . . .') rarely get you very far. Mostly, they go down with teenagers like a lead balloon. It's much better to be specific, answer questions straight and honestly, have a bit of sympathy or use a little psychology where necessary.

The good parent takes the middle way. Would you let your son or daughter of 15 bring their girl- or boyfriend home to sleep with them for the night? I wouldn't. It's my house and if they were 18 I might think about it, but at 15 I just couldn't agree to that. Do you let your 13-year-old son watch horror movies or sex and horror videos until the early hours of the morning? I wouldn't. Parents have a right to say, 'This is not doing your physical or mental health much good. I'm not having it.'

Do you talk to your teenagers, quietly and sensibly about

sex? Have you told them about the dangers of casual sex? What would you do if you found out that your 14-year-old daughter was sleeping with her boyfriend? I wouldn't rant and rave at her, destroy her character, call her a slut. I'd deal with the situation as it is and make sure, if she's determined to sleep with her young man, that she saw the family doctor so that she could go on the pill. I think 14 is, from an emotional point of view, far too young to sleep with anyone. Nevertheless, if that is the situation it has to be dealt with. You can discuss the morality and the drawbacks of it later. The worst thing she can do is to irresponsibly bring an unwanted baby into the world. That has to be faced up to, and shouting at her, calling her a slag, won't solve the problem.

Everything I have said so far applies to the single parent as it does to those families which have two parents at home. What we've been discussing is an open and honest style of parenting in which negotiation and co-operation take the place of domination and abuse. I've emphasised that teenagers should contribute: if you expect nothing from them, that's what you'll get. I've stressed common sense, moving from love to friendship, and making sure that teenagers contribute something to the home. I've emphasised that trust, and treating them as response-able human beings, is vital, as is treating them differently according to their place in the family and their own abilities and interests.

Now, in the following chapters I want to deal with the world Out There, with the pressures on teenagers from school, from their own peer group, from unemployment and the complex business of growing up in today's world. I want to discuss pot smoking, football hooliganism, sexual relationships and the social world of the teenager. How far do you interfere and how far do you leave them to learn by their own mistakes? Many of us are puzzled by what approach to take with teenagers. We're not sure if we're being strict enough and, conversely, we know that to be repressive and domineering is no way to steer them towards maturity and independence. It isn't easy for parents of teenagers these days. In my view, it's harder than it's ever been.

There is very little agreement in our society as to what

values and lifestyle should be adhered to, little agreement as to what rules should be imposed, on what issues we parents must say no and speak up loudly and clearly for what we believe in. We're not always wrong, but to be fair to the teenagers neither are they. They have to tread their way through a minefield of choices and decisions. We have to give them the self-respect to make the right choices.

There was an experiment some years ago in which three groups of young people were each given a leader. One was an autocrat ('Do as I say'). One was a *laissez-faire* leader ('Do pretty much as you like'). The third was a democratic leader ('Let's talk about this and try to decide what to do'). It was the third group, in which the members of the group were consulted about decisions made and involved in what was decided that achieved most, best worked together without acrimony, and which came up with the best solutions to the problems they had to solve.

Love isn't enough. Teenagers really do need practice in negotiation. They have to be given information on the options open to them. They have to be treated as though they and their opinions and views are worth listening to. We have to learn to be democratic; they have to learn that other people count besides themselves. Then we work towards real friendship. Friends like and respect each other, they give back to us what we give to them. Teenagers and parents *can* be friends. It just takes an approach which is democratic and gives teenagers real responsibility in the running of their own lives.

Let's see how that works out in practice as we look at the teenager in his or her world outside the home. The modern world is a rapidly changing place. I don't envy teenagers trying to make sense of it all and trying to come through it with a strong belief in who they are and what they stand for.

'Love 'em and let 'em be' is what you must do with teenagers. Let's see how that love expresses itself in practical terms, and let's see how far you can go in letting 'em be; how much responsibility you can give them for their own lives. I've said I'm glad I'm not a teenager today; I mean it. They have some tricky problems to solve.

5
The school

I visited a friend's house last night. As we were chatting, his 14-year-old daughter was doing her homework. She was lying on the carpet, eating crisps, watching the television and drawing a map of England in an exercise book. That brought back memories.

My youngest daughter used to do her homework in much the same way. French translation, watching *Blue Peter*, eating biscuits and painting her toenails pink, all at the same time.

'Quelle heure est-il?' I'd ask her.

'Il fait beau,' she'd say.

What I want to do here is to give some practical advice about your teenager at school. I, like you, know that the school's influence is not as great as the home's. The home is there before your child ever goes to school and remains there when the child has left school. Many youngsters who don't do well at school go on to live successful and happy lives. Having said that, we all have to admit that school is important. We all spend eleven years of our lives at school, and we leave with a feeling of failure or achievement. I'd like to feel that every teenager leaves school with an enhanced, and not a diminished, self-respect.

Education, according to Matthew Arnold, is the influence of one person on another. Education, according to me, starts when you're born and ends when you die. It involves personal, social and vocational aspects. It is to do with the intellect, the emotions and the spirit. Good education enhances a person's self-esteem and gives them a sense of wonder at the beautiful world we live in, together with respect for other people. A truly educated person never stops learning, never ceases to be amazed by the wonder of the world, and never doubts that he or she has a right to walk the earth, with a sense of belonging, curiosity and self-regard.

What we've learned from educational research over the last forty years is that the influence of the home is paramount. The child, the school and the home form a triangle. Where the school has the most beneficial effect is when parents work with the school in the interests of the child. Schoolteachers (and headmasters and headmistresses) are not Martians. They are there for the benefit of the pupils in their charge. They do their most effective work when they have the support and co-operation of parents.

I know what you're thinking. Primary schools are, by and large, quite friendly places (though I knew one once with a sign in the playground saying NO PARENTS BEYOND THIS POINT). Secondary schools are different. They tend to be large, impersonal places with a lot of teachers and (you may think) a remote headmaster or headmistress. You may consider that a visit to such a place would be a very daunting experience indeed.

I remember when my mother visited my northern grammar school for the first time. She was there to discuss with the headmaster whether I should go into the sixth form or not. When she came back she said, 'He was ever so friendly. He gave me a cup of tea. He was quite human, really.' I think she expected the head to be a Creature from Outer Space, one of those Martians.

Some secondary schools, now, have open access for parents. All have parents on the governing body, many have a parent–teacher association, or a friends of the school association. Many have parent–teacher evenings and open evenings (or open days). Many have begun to involve parents in fund-raising events and out-of-school activities to enhance the experience of their pupils.

I'm not asking you to be a school governor. Perhaps you're a bit shy, don't think you'd have much to say. I have been one and it's a very rewarding experience. I'm not even asking you to join the PTA committee (unless you want to). I've done that, too: helped to organise jumble sales, school fêtes and parent–teacher evenings. It's great fun, you make friends, even if you're only part of the tea-making team. You also find out that teachers (and headmasters and head-mistresses) are human.

What I am asking you to do, throughout your teenager's school career, is to keep in touch with the school. If you have any doubts about your child's school work or his or her adjustment to school, do ring up the school secretary and ask for an appointment to see the youngster's form teacher or the teacher in charge of his or her tutor group. The school and the home should never become two worlds. When that happens it can only be to the detriment of the teenager.

I mentioned that business about homework for a purpose. I was worried about it and I went to see my daughter's form tutor.

'Her work's fine,' she told me. 'No problem.'

I ceased to worry about 14-year-olds doing four things at once. When my daughter went into her next year at school, she started to do her homework in the bedroom, where there was more peace and quiet and no television or nail varnish. They have to do it. We can't do it for them. What we can do is take practical steps when we think that things are going wrong.

You should contact the school, and ensure you go to the school to discuss matters, if your teenager shows sudden deterioration or loss of interest in his or her school work, if you suspect that your youngster is being bullied at school, if your youngster has no friends at school or doesn't seem to be settling down and shows no enthusiasm for school. Find out what's going on. It's your duty (and your right) as a parent.

Let me give you a simple example of effective school–parent liaison. When I was an educational psychologist, I was asked to see a 15-year-old boy who was playing truant from school. I chatted with him and he told me , 'I hate the place.' I found out that what he hated was maths. He felt 'stupid' during maths lessons and felt he could never keep up with the rest of the class. His hatred of maths and dislike of the maths teacher had generalised into a hatred of the school and all its teachers.

I visited the school, had a word with the maths teacher. He had no idea what was happening. We came to an arrangement whereby the boy did special maths work, set for him, where there was no pressure on him. The lad did two more geography lessons per week and two less maths lessons. The main thing was to get the youngster back to school and doing subjects that he enjoyed. We could sort out the maths later (which we did). The maths teacher was no monster: he simply didn't know what anxiety his subject aroused in the teenager concerned.

Next, the parents visited the school.

'Maths isn't the beginning and end of the world,' the maths teacher told them.

Everyone knew what the problem was. The problem, with co-operation and parental support, was sorted out. That lad, poor at maths, now runs his own business. The last time I saw him he told me how much he earned. It was more than his former headmaster! The moral is clear. Where something is wrong at school, do something about it. The school exists for the pupils, and parents and teachers exist to further the interests of the young people they teach.

If your youngster has no friends at school, a good teacher can always find a role for him or her, something special, which will boost the teenager's standing amongst his or her peers. If there is a marked deterioration in school work, it may be because your youngster has decided that he or she isn't respected at the school, that his or her own interests are not being developed, that he or she isn't being treated as a person. The only way you can find out is by discussing the situation quietly and calmly and working together with the school in your child's best interests.

Sometimes, teenagers have emotional problems which affect their school work. Most schools have teachers who assume a counselling role; every school has access to an educational psychologist who is trained to deal with the emotional problems (and who can refer the youngster to a Family Guidance Clinic if he or she thinks it necessary). We all pay for these services, and psychologists are not witch doctors. What, to you, is an insurmountable problem is, to them, part of their day-to-day work. Do ask the headmaster or headmistress, or your GP, if you can see the educational psychologist if you feel you cannot deal with your youngster's problem alone or you think that emotional factors are seriously upsetting your youngster's performance in school.

Why try to solve a problem by yourself when there is professional and confidential help available?

I once saw a 15-year-old girl who disliked school intensely. The teachers wrote things on her report like 'lazy', 'doesn't concentrate'. (Are these remarks an indication, I wonder, of a poor pupil or bad teaching?) I arranged for the girl to help out, two mornings a week, at a local playgroup. 'Marvellous,' the playgroup leader wrote of her to the headmistress. 'J. is brilliant with children. She's the best helper we've ever had.' There's something wrong here. Two views: one bad, one good. Same youngster.

What is the point of keeping in touch with the school? It is to make sure your youngster gets a square deal educationally, to discuss together what he or she is good at, so that teachers and parents together can discover the child's strengths, build upon them, help the youngster with his or her academic weak points in an encouraging and not discouraging way. That's what education is all about. We're not all academics. We can't all be professors (and wouldn't want to be). Every youngster has her or his strengths, good points. *The job of the school and of the parents is to find out what those strengths are, develop them and make sure that no youngster, yours or mine, leaves school with anything other than an enhanced self-regarding sentiment.*

Let's get down to brass tacks, to study, to homework and to the anxiety topic of exams. A teenager once told me: 'Homework is just part of life, isn't it? Like bee stings.' I firmly believe it is often excessive. 'It's just something that has to be done' (teachers claim) 'to cover the curriculum'. Whether young people should do such a lot of homework is something I don't intend to discuss here. Given that most teenagers have to do *some* homework, the question I want to answer is, what is the best way of setting about it?

I suggest that you:

● *Get your philosophy right.*
  Tell your teenager: 'It's less hassle to do it than to sit there worrying about it.' That's true (and true of other situations in life too).

- *Encourage a routine.*
  Homework to be done at a certain time each evening (depending on your meal-time). Television off if it spoils concentration. Older teenagers who work in their bed-rooms should be given a simple bench or table to work at and should get used to going upstairs to do their homework during the school term.

- *Discuss homework with the school,*
  especially if your youngster is having difficulty with it. What you want to know is what it's for and why that particular homework is set. Ask your youngster's teacher's advice on the best way to tackle the homework and what the school is hoping to achieve from it. Don't let your youngster work it out for him- or herself if the homework is confusing or too hard.

- *Save some time for your family to be together.*
  Homework has to be done, but it doesn't have to dominate family life. Save some evenings and weekends when you can do things together as a family and when homework doesn't dominate the proceedings.

- *Go to the school and see the teacher if the homework is causing chronic strain.*
  (Either in your youngster or in the family.) Homework is important, but it's not more important than family life and too much (or ill-thought-out homework) can put a teenager and his or her family under stress.

- *Make sure that older teenagers, working for exams, have somewhere quiet to work, away from the family hustle and bustle.*
  Keep the television down and have some consideration for them.

These are the main points. You may have a youngster who has a hobby, a skill, a particular talent which takes up his or her time out of school. My younger daughter was in the British Gymnastics Squad. At one time during her teenage years she used to practise gym for three hours on five evenings a week! Sometimes interests and special talents (for example music, sport, dancing) can take up a great deal of the youngster's spare time.

The main thing is to tell the school about it so that they make allowances for the youngster to develop these special skills. Also, remember that young people need time relaxing so that they can develop social skills, so do work closely with the school over homework. It has to be done, but it's hardly fair to expect a young person to work for six hours at school and follow that by another one to four hours in the evening! It has to be done (we're told) in order to pass exams, but do make sure that your teenager takes definite time off to relax and get some fresh air. Homework should not totally dominate your youngster's life.

One more point. What takes one child half an hour to do may take another two hours (and a great deal of sweat and anxiety). Homework must be appropriate to the age of the child and his or her ability. That's why you must keep in touch with the school to ask what it's for, what it's meant to achieve, and whether it's appropriate for your teenager. He or she will still have to do it, but at least the whole aim of it will be clearer. Then, you can say, 'Time for your homework,' and know that it makes sense and your teenager will know that you truly do sympathise. After all, you had to do it. Homework, like bee stings, is part of life. When it's done with family support, and dealt with routinely and sensibly, it's a great deal less painful.

Let's talk about habits of study. Some young people can work in a noisy atmosphere, others need peace and quiet. Some like to come home, get the work done, and relax. Others don't seem to start until about 9 pm and then emerge bleary-eyed in the morning, having been up until midnight. That's all right. If the style of working suits them (and they don't get over-tired from it), that's fine. There are larks and owls among teenagers as well as adults: some teenagers seem to settle down to work when the rest of the family is thinking of going to bed.

What I think is useful to know is that study doesn't have to consist of reading and writing. Some young people have a good auditory rather than visual memory. For them, a tape recorder may be a very good way of learning, of remembering facts, of preparing for an exam. One teenager will want to learn alone. Another may learn more by working with a friend on a given project: they can then discuss the work together and actively set about finding answers (or help each other to 'swot up' for a test).

The principle of active learning is vital. It's no use a teenager sitting there daydreaming, pretending to read a book. It's much better to write things down, draw sketches, diagrams, or resort to various other methods of remembering material. To learn most effectively, it's important to be organised and to have definite goals.

How to Succeed at GCSE by John Bowden (Cassell) is a useful book for teenagers and parents. It's very readable and deals with many of the difficulties teenagers have in working for GCSE.

Say your youngster is coming up to GCSE or some other important examination. What is the best way of preparing for an exam? I suggest that your teenager should:

Have a definite plan of revision. Do a given amount of work each evening and use a tape recorder if he or she has a poor visual memory. Record the main facts and play the tape (even in the bathroom) until they're known. A Sony Walkman might be a good idea to save strain on the other members of the family!

Learn main points. Use cards (to jot down main headings), wall charts, small notebooks, graphs. Use mnemonics (e.g. KNITTING, a mnemonic I used at school to remember the causes of the French Revolution. It reminded me that the King was weak, the Nobles corrupt, the Intellectuals dissatisfied, and so on.) I sincerely hope that schools over the next decade move away from imparting esoteric or useless facts to their pupils. I learned the causes of the French Revolution and the details of the Treaty of Utrecht many years ago. Nobody has ever asked me about them since, and I've often wondered about the use of such information. Richard Of York Gained Battles In Vain is a way of remembering the colours of the rainbow (red, orange, yellow, green, blue, indigo, violet), and many of us know the rhyme 'Thirty days hath September, April, June and November. All the rest have thirty-one, except February . . .' This has helped me since I was a child to remember how many days there are in each month. Mnemonics can be useful in organising facts.

Look at old exam papers and have a go at some of the questions. Use an alarm clock to time how long it takes. Work with a friend, if preferred. The main thing is to know how much time is available and be prepared for those time limits in the real exam.

Never leave revision until the last minute. Start, say, three months in advance; work steadily until the exam gets near. At this stage, revise headings and main points. Try not to go into the exam over-tired or panicky.

When the exam is there, make sure of the time and place of the exam. Have two pens (one in reserve). Read the instructions on the exam paper carefully. Plan answers, answering easier questions first if necessary to gain confidence, and leaving sufficient time for other questions.

Leave ten minutes at the end of the exam to check through answers. Correct any silly mistakes or spelling errors. (These lose marks, so the last ten minutes doing this is well spent.)

During exam time many youngsters feel enormous strain. You may spot yours going upstairs, white-faced, to do his or her 'swotting' after a hastily-eaten tea. Have sympathy, but don't pick up his or her anxiety. 'You're working hard,' is a good thing to say. Remain calm and supportive. Say 'Good luck,' as he or she goes off in the morning. 'Do your best,' you could say.

Be encouraging. Have a special treat at meal-times or at the weekend. Show that you care about what a straining time it is. That's what it's about. They have to go in there and do it, you have to try to remain as calm and supportive as you can through this very harrowing time. Make sure your youngster gets enough sleep and eats well, then cross your fingers and hope that they do themselves justice. That's all we can do, though we'd like to do more. Exams are also like bee stings: part of the sharp edge of life.

A great many parents ask me about handwriting. 'My son's writing is indecipherable,' is a typical comment. 'What can I do about it?' All three of my own youngsters went through a stage when their handwriting was *terrible*. What we did was to buy each of them in turn a Platignum fountain pen with an italic nib. We then bought them *Handwriting* by Tom Gourdie MBE (Ladybird Books). The modified italic style advocated in the book is easy to learn and 'tidies up' handwriting like a charm. Youngsters should start off by doing small amounts of writing in their new style. This way they learn to enjoy it, take a pride in their handwriting, and start to write more quickly and neatly.

What about spelling? I personally can't spell for toffee. I always keep a dictionary by the side of my desk and resort to it frequently. Why not? That's what dictionaries are for. Does spelling matter (you may ask)? I think it does. An essay riddled with spelling mistakes is not likely to impress examiners, and future employers will expect correct spelling. A useful little book is Fred Schonell's *The Essential Word Spelling List* (Macmillan). This inexpensive book groups words into families (e.g. the *kn* words: *kn*it, *kn*ot, *kn*ock, *kn*ee), and the youngster is able to see the pattern of words: those which have the same beginnings or endings. There are plenty of other books to help young people to spell; some are listed at the back of this book. These, and the frequent use of a dictionary, can take all the misery out of spelling. It doesn't *have* to be a chore. Even if you are a naturally bad speller like me, spelling can be fun, and correct spelling makes a letter or any other written piece of work more presentable to the reader.

Up to now my advice has been concerned with the nuts and bolts of learning. I'd like, at this stage, to say something about some wider issues. Education is to do with character, with all-round development, with the emotions as well as the intellect; it has a vocational and spiritual aspect. So let's look at some of these less specific, though no less vital aspects of the teenager's life at school.

Consider sex education. Years ago a headmaster said to me: 'I don't want sex education in my school. My boys don't get pregnant.' To me, that betrays a fundamental misunderstanding of what sex education is about. It's about relationships, about feelings, about respect for others, about caring for other people. It involves boys as well as girls. It is to do with the whole person, with parenthood, with family life in general.

Imagine a talk on 'sex education' as it might, or once did, happen. The expert enters, carrying a box of contraceptives, which she or he proceeds to show to the class. There are giggles, nudges, winks. The speaker pulls no punches, tells the class exactly what the various items do, how they're used, what they're for.

What's wrong with this approach? It deals with the physical aspects of sex in isolation, outside the context of love, of caring relationships and the family. It ignores the wide variation in the sexual and emotional maturity of the pupils present. It often implies that girls and not boys are primarily responsible for the relationship (including contraception). It ignores the religious and deeply-held personal views of young people regarding sex which should be discussed in the general context of our relationships with other people. It may undermine the parents' sincerely held views on the whole question of young people having sex, or having sex before marriage.

The best judges of a youngster's maturity in these matters are usually his or her parents. Teenagers in school do have to be given balanced and appropriate information on sexual matters in the context of caring relationships and know something of the changes in attitude towards sexual behaviour that have taken place over the years. You, as a parent, have a right to know why, when and how sex education is approached in your teenager's school. Every school should have a clearly formulated sex education policy and you, as a parent, ought to know what that policy is.

If you don't know, you must ask. You could ask for a parent evening to discuss what the goals and the method of achieving them are. These days it's dangerous for young people to have casual sex. The problem of AIDS and other sexually transmitted diseases is one that cannot be ignored. At the same time, we have to bear in mind that sex ought to be looked at in the context of preparation for parenthood and responsible relationships. These are all vital issues, and I think you ought to take an interest in them and know what the approach is in the school so that it doesn't contradict the approach to these matters taken in the home. (There is more about *your* attitude to sex on pages 93–4.)

I wish that more schools would make a definite commitment to the education of the emotions. Emotions (from the Latin *ē*, from, and *movere*, to move) are the things that move, motivate, human beings: they are the engine room of the personality. Geography and history are important, but so are drama, dance, painting, sculpture, music, woodwork, weaving, pottery. It is through media like these that we can learn to express our feelings of happiness, sadness, joy, frustration, anger and sorrow.

Our emotional attitude to problems greatly affects our chances of solving them. To have outlets for the intellect but not for the emotions is to be half-educated. A normal as well as a maladjusted youngster gets an enormous amount of reassurance and reward from expressing emotions through paint, through acting, through movement. What is the point of educating young people to be 'clever' if we never teach them how to express the emotions that are within them?

I spent 13 years at school. I can give you the details of the French revolution; I cannot read or play a note of music (though music is one of my great loves). I cannot sculpt, paint, weave, sew or express myself in any other medium save writing. That is what I call a lopsided education. It is to know that they have coffee in Brazil but not know how to crochet a tie or be able to play a simple tune on the piano or the recorder.

For any youngster, at any age, what we should be concerned with is the whole person, with the Physical, Intellectual, Emotional and Social aspects of that person's being (it's easy to remember: think of PIES). Remember that a great deal of education takes place in the family, in the street, in the neighbourhood, in the school holidays. Schools are not the only places that educate children.

To encourage teenagers' special interests and hobbies or special talents is to widen their repertoire of abilities and prepare them for the world after they have left school. I have known quite a few young people who have converted a special talent or a hobby into a full-time job on leaving school.

One young woman, mad about art at school, now has her own business making greetings cards. I've met youngsters interested in computers, cooking, car mechanics, motorbikes, weaving, knitting, cooking and pastry-making all working in their own area of special interest now that they have left school. One young woman, devoted to dancing, now runs her own dancing school. Another, besotted with horses, works in a riding stables. A young man who taught himself how to play the guitar accompanies pop stars on world tours, and makes a great deal more money than you or I.

Once your child reaches the stage at secondary school where he or she has to choose which subjects to take for exams, or which job he or she would like to aim for, the decisions involved should be taken by the child and a partnership of home and school. If everybody works closely together, then the chances are that the youngster will head in a direction which he or she wants and which both parents and school are happy about. Does your teenager want to go to college or become a hair stylist or work in a bank or work in a library? At the appropriate stage you will need to know what qualifications are needed for a particular choice, and you and the school must realistically assess what goals your teenager can set for him- or herself.

I must stress the notion of partnership between home and school. When I was the chairman of my eldest daughter's secondary school PTA, we ran a jumble sale. On the Friday evening (the jumble sale was the next day) I knocked on the door of the mother of one of the girls at the school. She was a single parent and very shy.

I got her to promise that she would come the next afternoon to help with making the tea at the jumble sale. She didn't turn up. (Looking back, I know that somebody should have gone to collect her and she'd probably have come.) She was too shy, very diffident, scared that we'd all be stand-offish and unfriendly.

Quite a few parents feel like that. They are daunted by the prospect of visiting a secondary school: it reminds them too much of their own schooldays. Things, though, *have* changed. Schools are much more open now, much more interested in the idea of the education of the teenager as a partnership between school and home.

That is why, without being over-anxious, too interfering or bossy, you must take an interest in the secondary education of your youngster from day one. What is the policy of the school regarding uniforms, discipline, caning? Does the school have counsellors who can help with the educational or emotional problems of pupils? Does the school have a PTA? To what aspects of the school life can a parent make a valid, helpful contribution?

Education *is* the influence of one person on another. That includes you, the parent. Education is as wide as the ocean. Education is life. It is to do with curiosity and character and courage. It is to do with learning how to lead life to the full.

Even in these days of high unemployment, when the voc-ational aspects of secondary education have come to the foreground, we still cannot say education is *only* about jobs, a career. Krishnamurti, the Eastern mystic and teacher (*Krishnamurti Reader*, edited by Mary Lutyens [Penguin Books 1973]), says of education:

> Having a job and earning one's livelihood is necessary – but is that all? Are we being educated only for that? Surely, life is not merely a job, an occupation . . . life is much more important than merely prepare for examinations and become very proficient in mathematics, physics or what you will.

Though it may seem amiss to point this out with so many young people unemployed, Krishnamurti is right. I've met more than one young person, brilliant academically, having been to university (some of them to Oxford or Cambridge where they have gained outstanding degrees), who have said to me in their twenties, 'I am desperately unhappy.' That is because their education has been too focused, too narrowly academic. It has ignored the emotional and social aspects, which are vital. It has made young people feel that they are respected or loved for what they have achieved (in this case academically) rather than for what they are.

That is wrong. Every young person is unique. Our job as parents and teachers is to bring out the best in them and develop what they have to offer. Every young person is special. Everybody on the class register ought to count, not just the 'clever' youngsters.

Young people are not blackboards on which we scribble our theories. They are not containers that we cram to the brim with facts. They are human beings, with their own aspirations, dreams and hopes. They may not make their dreams come true, but we must never put them down nevertheless. Education, if it does anything, fills people with curiosity, enthusiasm and wonder. It lights fires in young souls; it doesn't dampen the spirit. It enables, not disables.

What is education? It is learning to live. In that worthwhile enterprise you, as a parent, have a vital part to play. You must:

- *Take an interest in your youngster's education.*
  Parental interest and encouragement *do* affect a teenager's achievement in school.

- *Remember there are late developers who succeed in life rather than at school.*
  Don't criticise your child if he or she is non-academic. Do find out what he or she *is* good at and encourage and develop that talent.

- *Avoid saying things like, 'You're hopeless at French.'*
  If he or she is, so what? Accentuate the positive. Say, 'You're doing very well at English.' That's encouragement. Criticism and putting people down doesn't work.

- *Remember that character, and the ability to get on with people, are just as important as academic brightness in the long journey through life.*
  Winston Churchill was hopeless at school lessons. He, presumably, had parents who didn't tell him he was hopeless as a person.

- *Avoid being arrogant with your youngster.*
  Education today is education for change, a preparation for living in the twenty-first century. Don't tell them things were different and better in your day. Learn alongside them and *listen* when they tell you about school. You may learn something yourself.

- *Liaise and co-operate with the school, right from the start, in the best interests of your child.*
  Arrange to visit the school if you're worried or puzzled over homework, an aspect of the curriculum, a behaviour problem. The teachers are there to serve the best interests of pupils. Parents and teachers together are the base on which your youngster will achieve most from the school.

- *Join in the school activities for parents.*
  Help out at various events. Join the PTA. Become a parent governor. Why not? I made a lot of friends among other parents when my children were at secondary school. You will too if you join in, regard the school as a place for parents as well (and not a corrective training establishment or a branch of the Noise Abatement Society).

- *Remember education means learning for living.*
  If you take an active interest in your youngster's education, you will educate yourself as you're taking part.

- *Call in specialist help if you need it.*
  For academic or emotional crises, the help is there and, through the school, you can avail yourself of it. There is nothing that a school and parents cannot sort out if they work together in the interests of the youngster concerned.

6
Teenage problems in today's world

I'm not going to be dogmatic about the issues I intend to discuss in the next few pages. They're serious issues and you, as a parent, must make up your own mind on how to approach them. What I believe is that teenagers, like adults, have to make a series of choices in today's confusing world. In order to make the right choices they need the facts, and those facts have to be given progressively. They have to take into account the teenager's age and stage: his or her level of maturity. Your aim, always, is to make your teenager a self-respecting human being and one who shows respect for the rights of others.

SEX

Take sex. A woman friend of mine told me that she was 18 when she first found out the meaning of the word 'penis'. Another woman friend told me that her sex education consisted of her mother pointing to the mantelpiece and saying, 'There's a little book on there I think you ought to read.' Sex was never mentioned in the house again. One woman I know started her periods at the age of 12 having been told nothing whatsoever about menstruation. She said the experience was 'terrifying'.

Simple information on biological functions and on sexual relationships can save a great deal of anxiety, distress and worry. Teenagers need information on sexual matters. They need to be reassured that they are 'normal' if they think about sex. They need to be able to discuss body hygiene and to know they can talk to somebody if they have a rash or period

89

pains, or are confused about what gays do to each other or what happens to the umbilical cord after a baby is born.

You may be a parent who has answered your child's questions about sex openly and briskly since he or she was an infant. That's fine. You'll continue as you started, being honest and open about the subject. (Though you'll still feel a mixture of surprise and disbelief that your erstwhile little girl is now an attractive sexual being and cuddles her boyfriend on the sofa! How did she grow up so soon?)

You may be a parent who is embarrassed to talk about sex with your teenager. I hope you'll overcome this embarrassment and try your best to give them the facts that they need. Every teenager has a list of Things I Wish I Knew. Why not tell them? I think they deserve the truth and, if you are open and honest about sex (about what you know and what you *don't* know), your teenager will confide in you. If you're evasive (or pretend to know everything), they will spot that and cease to trust you.

Consider the teenager's position in today's world. On television, in magazines, in certain newspapers, there's a 'laid-back', casual attitude to sex. The message seems to be, 'Do it if you want to.' Magazines contain photos of men and women in 'sexy' poses. There are those page three photographs of semi-naked women. What is a teenager to make of it all? In school or in the family there may be a quite different attitude to sex. Some parents will want their teenagers to stick to the values of chastity, fidelity and sex within marriage. Other parents may have strong religious beliefs. The poor teenager has to weave his or her way through these opposing views of what sex is all about.

This is why honesty from parents is so vital. If you think sex should be part of a loving relationship, say so. Sex is always contextual. It takes place under a railway bridge, at a party with someone you don't know; or it takes place within a faithful, loving relationship with somebody that you care for deeply; or it takes place within marriage. You will have your own views on this and you are entitled to voice those views.

When you talk to your teenager about sex, don't be strident, bombastic, bossy (and don't duck out of awkward questions and say, 'Ask your father about that'). Say what you think. There is nothing 'dirty' about sex. If you, as a parent, give the unspoken message that sex is shameful and nasty, then you are adding to the confusion that the teenager may already feel about the subject. It's not your answers but your attitude which is most important.

As I said before, you should find out what your teenager's school is doing about sex education. Does your teenager attend sex education lessons? Is he or she taught about simple sexual hygiene, sexual relationships, love and friendship, gay relationships? Are there any aspects of such lessons which worry you or go against the values you are trying to instil at home? If so, you must go up to the school and explain your point of view. A good school will always respect family opinions.

What I would say is that *somebody* has to give teenagers the facts. I don't mean the 'sex lady' coming into the classroom bearing a tray of contraceptives and talking about VD. I don't mean sex education books that talk about sex but never mention love. I mean a full discussion of sex as part of a loving relationship. I mean responsibility towards oneself and others. I mean telling teenagers about life, about what responsibility towards others really means. That's real sex education, and you should ensure that your teenager is given sex education by a skilled teacher and in the context of human relationships. Information without an emphasis on caring relationships can be alarming to teenagers (and parents).

What about your own role, as a parent? I think it is to be honest and to give such facts as you can. You can tell your youngster about when you were a teenager, your boyfriends or girlfriends, your first love, the pain of being chucked for someone else, how mad you were about a certain film star or pop star. Don't make out you were the Torvil and Dean of the sexual ice-rink. Talk about your hopeless loves, the time he (or you) didn't turn up, the mistakes, the fun and the pain. That's the human context. It's the love that counts, and love is more than sex.

You can talk about feelings. What it felt like when you were in love for the first time, who your first boyfriend or girlfriend was, what he or she was like, what you fancied about him or her. That's interesting to teenagers. They're often astonished to find that other people, including parents, have been in love too. You can tell something of your own experiences as a teenager to your own 13-year-old or 18-year-old. Human relationships are always interesting, providing you're not too didactic or trying to prove a point.

I told my three youngsters about when I was a teenager and how I lay in bed with a torch and a diagram of a girl's bra, trying to figure out how to undo the wretched thing. What with bras constructed like the Bank of England and hooped, crinoline petticoats, the problem for teenage boys in my day was terminal exhaustion.

'The female body was a complete mystery to us,' I told them. A slight exaggeration. All I wanted them to know was that we could all talk about sex without a deathly hush spreading over the whole house.

Some parents will have talked to their youngsters and answered questions briskly and openly since the children were young. Some, as I've said, have a natural shyness about the subject and find it difficult to discuss. That's fine. We're not all the same. What we must try to do is give our opinions on the subject quietly, firmly, without being bombastic and sanctimonious. We must get across to our youngsters that they can say 'no' to sex if they want to. We must give them the facts that will enable them to come to the right decisions.

Young teenagers need to be given the facts about contraception. Many young teenage girls say no, stay chaste, don't sleep with their boyfriends. Some young teenage girls do sleep with their boyfriends. If you, as a parent, discover that your daughter is sleeping with her boyfriend, it doesn't help to call her wicked or a slut. The sensible thing is to go to your family doctor and ensure that she is using effective contraception. (The family doctor will advise on this.) Your practical help may be of more use than a moral sermon or rejecting your daughter out of hand as a slag.

All teenagers need to know about venereal disease. If they know the facts, it gives them the choice. They may choose not to sleep with anybody, or to sleep with a long-term, committed and faithful partner. Either way, they avoid catching VD. They reduce the risk, if they do choose to have casual sex, if they wear a sheath or condom. To indulge in casual sex these days without using a sheath is very dangerous. The sexual risks of 'sleeping around' are very real indeed.

You, as a parent, have a duty to ensure that your youngster has been given the sexual facts at school. If he or she hasn't, then you can obtain information from the Health Education Council or from the Family Planning Association. Certainly no youngster should, these days, leave school and go out into the world knowing nothing about AIDS, about VD (gonorrhoea and syphilis), or about Non-Specific Urethritis in men and Non-Specific Vaginitis in women. It is the right of every youngster to have access to the facts on these serious matters. We are talking about life, health and happiness, and they are serious matters indeed.

It isn't only a matter of information, though. There is a moral aspect. Take unwanted pregnancy. It can be prevented by a responsible attitude which does include a consideration of moral questions. You have an opportunity, as a parent, to put your views, quietly and without bombast, on certain issues which involve choice, judgement and values. If you have certain values, why not say what they are? At least that gives your youngster a chance to know what you think about various things.

I saw a TV programme recently in which a group of teenage girls, unemployed and unmarried, had deliberately chosen to have babies. This was pregnancy out of choice. It gave the girls something to do, someone to love. The fact that they were now mothers gave these girls a daily programme of activity. Having a baby gave some meaning to their lives.

What I discussed with friends after the TV programme were a series of questions. Was it fair on the babies? Will they be brought up in an atmosphere of love? Will the babies be loved as much when they are older? Do these young mothers know that rearing a child to maturity is a rough, tough and lifelong business? These are the sort of questions that I'd like to see teenagers, girls and boys, discussing in school.

What about abortion? Is it ever right? If it is, under what circumstances? These are the sorts of problems that teenagers are interested in and ought to have a chance of discussing. Sex education isn't just biology. It concerns the emotions, respect for others, moral choices and respect for ourselves. Young people need to be told that it's OK to be chaste, OK to say no to sex (and that it *is* possible for a girl to be respected by boys for *not* doing it). Sex isn't compulsory.

Boys, particularly, ought to be given a Men Too philosophy. That men, too, have responsibility in these matters. That men, too, have to learn respect for others and for themselves. With sex education there must be no sex discrimination. What is responsible sex for Gloria is responsible sex for Graham. It's no use teaching girls to behave responsibly if we don't teach boys the same thing.

So do discuss sexual facts with your teenager (and if you don't know, help them to find the answer). Don't forget to discuss feelings. If you think that sleeping around is dangerous and does nothing at all for one's self-respect, say so. If you think that casual sex is morally wrong, say so. You have a right to say it; it's the way you say it that counts. Discuss it, put your point of view. Listen to your teenager's point of view. It's the open and frank atmosphere that you create in the home that makes the teenager not afraid to talk to you when he or she is frightened or confused.

Our job as parents with regard to sex is not to add to those fears. It is to help teenagers by the presentation of facts and sincere, undogmatic opinion to aid them through their confusion. Just be open and honest when they come to you. Never laugh at them or over-criticise them. You'll know, since you've been a teenager yourself, what a minefield teenage love can be. Remember your first love and don't let them down by pretending it wasn't painful for you. Talk about love, about friendship, about fancying people and having teenage crushes. That is the foundation of human relationships on which any discussion of sex ought to be based.

If you are very shy and find it hard to talk about these matters, that's all the more reason to ensure that the school, or a youth leader, or a sympathetic, trusted adult is available to talk to your teenager about the facts. If your youngster is afraid that he or she is sexually abnormal in some way, a word with a sympathetic GP or trusted adult can save months of worry and distress. We have to be tender when we talk to children about love and sex. We have to be tough about giving them the facts. They need those facts in order to gain self-respect and to make the right decisions.

You, as a parent, don't need to know everything about sex, nor do you need to pry into your youngster's sex life. Openness and honesty breed trust and, in the last analysis, you have to trust your teenager to make the right decisions. Most do, so have faith.

You have to be sensitive to teenage doubts and fears. Some teenagers will wonder whether they are gay, some will be distraught over a love affair which has just broken up, some may have a crush on an older boy or girl at school or on one of the masters or mistresses and be in despair about it, some will wonder whether they are sexually normal and be worried sick about some part of their anatomy or about their physical attractiveness. They may not want to talk to you as their parents about these private fears.

That's OK as long as we, as parents, mention to them (perhaps talking about other teenagers) that the Samaritans exist, and that one phone call has saved many a despairing teenager. We need to mention the local Citizens' Advice Bureau and the confidential help it provides. We can refer teenagers to the list of addresses given in the back of this book. We may not know the answer to their problems: somewhere, there is somebody who does. Our job as parents is to let teenagers know that there is confidential and free help available, whatever the problem, and to steer them in the direction of that help should they need it.

I consider it a human right for children to be educated about sex at school. I think that the sex education they need should include biological processes, but should also lay emphasis on wider social issues, on the emotional aspects of relationships and on the notion of self-respect and respect for others. The job of parents is to work with the school in these matters and to create an atmosphere in the home in which sex can be mentioned and is not taboo or nasty or shameful. We live in a society that, sometimes, seems to be obsessed with sex. It's parents that have to restore a measure of dignity to this awful degradation of what should be an expression of love between two human beings.

It's tough on parents. If you want to teach your teenagers about love and sex you must:

● *Be open about your own doubts, confusions and uncertainties.*
That takes courage.

● *Remember that sex is not an isolated topic.*
It belongs in a context of human relationships and respect for each other. How you show affection in the home, how you show your love, will affect your teenagers' attitude to sex and human relationships in general.

● *Inform not warn.*
Threats and warnings don't work. Information about and discussion of feelings, wants, needs and emotions do work. Warning young people off sex in an authoritarian way simply makes them want to experiment because they know you haven't told them the whole truth.

● *Get across that what they do (masturbate, have wet dreams, think about sex) is normal.*
So are puppy love, pashes, and crushes on older heroes and heroines. Say it happened to you. That's a very reassuring thing to hear.

● *Do not pretend to know it all.*
Stick up for what you believe in, say what you think and then listen to your teenager. You'll learn a lot. It's quite remarkable, considering the confused and crazy world we live in, just how sensible most teenagers are about sex. Maybe they have something to teach us!

- *Remember that first love happens only once.*
  Most of us never forget it. Have some sympathy when it happens to your son or daughter. Say: 'Love sometimes hurts.' It does. Say: 'Talk to me whenever you need to.' That's all you need to say.

- *Your job as a parent is to inform and support.*
  They'll make the right decisions, the right choices, if they know we trust them.

DRUGS

Exactly the same general approach applies to drugs. For parents, the two things they fear most are an unmarried teenage daughter becoming pregnant and a teenage son or daughter becoming a drug addict. As with sex, what counts most in dealing with the subject of drugs is *attitude*. The problem has to be faced openly and honestly, without being alarmist but without closing your eyes and hoping that the problem will go away and that your son or daughter will never come into contact, at any time, with drugs. The chances are that he or she will. It's what happens next that counts.

You as a parent will probably be very frightened of drugs, know little or nothing about them and have had no experience of smoking cannabis. The notion of your own youngster experimenting with 'pot' may well scare the life out of you, as would any thought that he or she would try stronger drugs like LSD, cocaine or heroin. I, too, share your fears on the subject. So what is the best way for parents to tackle it?

First, we have to understand why young people take drugs. There is no such thing as a typical 'junkie'. Drug users come from a variety of backgrounds, some rich, some poor. They include young people who are on the dole as well as youngsters who are at university or are in other ways high achievers. All young people can, if they try hard enough, find somebody who will sell them drugs. That's why it's important to urge youngsters to 'Just say no.'

Let's get the problem into some kind of perspective. It is difficult to stop the entry of drugs into the country. People are willing to risk being sent to gaol for smuggling in drugs. Addicts will always be tempted to deal in drugs to support their own habit. This means that the drugs are there, in pubs, discos, on street corners and at teenage parties. It's almost impossible to stop teenagers being exposed to the sale of drugs.

What happens out there in the street is a witness to the common sense of most teenagers. About one-fifth (i.e. 20 per cent) will try some form of drug-taking (usually, smoking 'grass' or 'pot', i.e. cannabis). They smoke a joint (or have a puff or two on it) and decide that there's nothing in it for them, they don't get much out of it, and they subsequently leave it alone. They try out cannabis and that's it (just as we, when young, would drink alcohol because it was there, available and forbidden).

The at-risk group amongst teenagers are the one-fiftieth (i.e. 2 per cent) who try hard drugs (e.g. LSD, heroin or cocaine). Heroin is known as 'skag' or 'smack'. A heroin user is known as a 'smack-head'. The heroin can be injected into a vein or 'popped' under the skin, or the powder can be heated and the smoke inhaled (this is known as 'chasing the dragon'). Heroin is highly addictive. There is no certainty about whether cocaine is addictive. (This is a white powder which is usually sniffed or inhaled – a practice known as 'snorting'.) It is certainly expensive, as is heroin. This is why drug addicts are drawn into crime, including drug pushing, to support, say, a heroin addiction which can cost them in excess of £200 per week.

Drug pushers know why young people take drugs. They take them for excitement, to take risks, to taste the forbidden. They respond to peer-group pressure and want to belong, to be one of the 'in-crowd'. This group, the experience seekers, are the largest group at risk. There will be a smaller group who will use drugs to seek oblivion, just as some adults use alcohol to seek exactly the same thing. Often, these young people feel unable to cope with the world. They feel depressed, inadequate, lonely. They take drugs to escape from their feelings. The trouble is, as with alcohol, when the effect of the drug has worn off the world is still there, waiting to be coped with (and so are the feelings of stress and inadequacy).

The third group at risk are those who are attempting to bring about a change in their personality, and in their effectiveness in human relationships, by the use of drugs. The truth is that the very shy, hostile, alienated or fearful youngster needs tuition and practice in social skills (i.e. in making friends, making a relationship with a member of the opposite sex, being 'popular'). Drugs are no short cut to the social success craved, nor will they fill the emptiness that the young drug user feels within him- or herself. Drugs are the road to oblivion, not the road out of it.

What you as a parent need to understand is that drugs (pills, solvents, LSD, cannabis, heroin and cocaine) are readily available. Prevention in these matters, as with many others, works better than cure. It's a good thing to say to your teenagers when the chance arises, that is when you're talking about drugs or there is something about drugs on TV, 'Anybody who takes drugs is a fool,' or 'Just say no.' It's the calm and matter-of-fact way you say it that counts.

Parents know that young teenagers who sniff glue or other solvents (paints, nail varnish, dry-cleaning fluids, degreasing compounds) can get those solvents if they wish. Like other drugs, they are readily available. That's why draconian warnings, panic and fear on the part of parents leading to threats, detailed descriptions of how glue sniffers can die by choking on their own vomit, how experimenting with 'soft' drugs leads on to experimentation with 'hard' drugs, simply don't work. It may be better to say, when the subject comes up: 'Drug-taking kills you eventually.' That's true.

What does help teenagers in their own fight against the drug culture which surrounds them are three things: communication, listening to them, and trying to understand their point of view. It's worth remembering that *all* teenagers can acquire drugs if they try. That includes pills ('uppers' e.g. 'Dexies', or 'downers' e.g. 'mandies' or valium), solvents, pot or hard drugs, so you have to know that *they* have the final say as to whether they take drugs or not. That 'no' to drugs has to come from inside *them*.

In communicating with your teenagers you have to be open and honest. If you smoke cigarettes you could say: 'It's a daft, expensive habit. It costs me £10 a week. That's £500 a year. I regret the day I took it up.' That's honest, and it's better than arguing that cigarettes do you no harm whilst heroin kills you. All drugs taken to excess will kill you. What your teenagers want from you is honesty and frankness, not a pack of lies or excuses.

If you drink you should admit that it, too, can become addictive. Don't try to be a hero or heroine with your teenager as the villain. You can still say, of glue sniffing: 'It gives you a hangover and it damages your liver and kidneys. Plus it can kill you.' That's true. It's also true of alcohol, but your teenager knows that two wrongs don't make a right. What he or she is interested in is whether, when you speak about drugs, you use common sense, tell the truth and don't resort to lies and threats. After all, the chances are that your teenager knows more about the subject than you do.

That's why you have to listen. You can say: 'It's so cynical. The people who benefit from drugs are the drug barons. They make vast profits, it seems to me, from manipulating young people.' Then, hear what your youngster has to say. If he or she says that alcohol or cigarette smoking is a much bigger problem, then don't deny it. There's plenty of truth in that (and it's a much bigger problem with young teenagers than soft or hard drugs). Most young people who try drugs do so on a 'drift in, drift out' basis. It's the parent who doesn't listen to what the teenager has to say (mostly, out of fear) who gives the subject a forbidden, taboo aura that makes drug experimentation seem more attractive, not less.

You must understand the materialism of our society, the fact that there are many youngsters who are unemployed. You must try to understand the feeling of living in a big city or in a small town without a job. That does breed alienation, but it needn't breed alienation from parents providing parents understand the harsh, confusing and money-orientated world in which teenagers live. Don't say things like, 'You lot are lazy, idle.' They're not. Don't say, 'Things were harder in my day.' They weren't. Say, 'I'm glad I'm not a teenager today. It's a baffling and tough world.' That indicates sympathy and a measure of understanding.

I once saw a teenager, aged about 16, walking through the middle of Liverpool. The area through which she was walking looked as though a bomb had just hit it. There was graffiti scrawled on walls, rubble everywhere. The young woman walked, head in the air, terribly pretty and neat, through all the desolation. She looked one of the most proud, attractive and 'together' young women I have ever seen.

Many teenagers adjust incredibly well in this confusing and dangerous world in which we live. Some teenagers (that one-fifth) will try drugs out of fear, excitement, danger, a need to belong. Teenagers will, most of them, be exposed to drugs at some time. Most of them will 'just say no', because they know it's stupid. Parents have to listen to teenagers if they want to talk about drugs and, by their calm and sensible, non-panicky approach, confirm that message. It *is* stupid.

What families of those teenagers who have become dependent on drugs must remember is that many teenagers *do* kick the habit and that there is help available. Parents can ring the local Drug Advisory Centre, or ask their Citizens' Advice Bureau whether there is an Aid for Addicts and Family (ADFAM) parent group in the area. They can write to Release to ask for help and advice with a drug-related problem. Some heroin addicts find that kicking the habit is not as bad as giving up cigarettes. The 'cold turkey' treatment is not as awful as has been depicted. Young people *can* come off heroin. The main thing is to find a group which will support them during and after their attempt to give up the drug.

You don't need to preach to your teenagers about drugs. Just tell them the truth if they bring up the subject. Drugs are not clever: they're stupid. People who take drugs are being taken for a ride by those people who profit from drugs. Drugs are no fun. They can lower functioning level, damage health, eventually (taken hard and long enough) kill you. They solve nothing. The brightness and 'happiness' they provide is phoney, false and very temporary. Drugs cost money which can be spent on things that add to, not detract from, self-respect. That's the truth about drugs.

To get that truth across, use an honest, open and un-bombastic approach. Say what you think but remember that your teenager has an opinion too. Listen. No dire warnings about drugs and the dreadful things they do to you. Just be matter-of-fact and tell your youngster what you know and leave it at that.

Check up on whether your teenager is told about drugs at school, and know what sort of approach they are taking. Don't make too much fuss about it, but it's right and proper that your teenager *is* told, sensibly and calmly, about the dangers of drugs. The symptoms of drug-taking, in my view (lethargy, mood swings, lack of concentration, sudden deterioration in school work, pallor, depression, weight loss), can be applied to many teenagers who don't take drugs.

If, however, you suspect that your youngster is on drugs, you should contact your local Drug Advisory Centre (or go along and have a word with your GP) and you will be advised as to the best way to handle the matter. Do take advice and *don't* accuse, threaten or otherwise pronounce a 'guilty' verdict on your youngster before you are sure. The way forward on drugs is to realise that it's a people problem, not a chemical problem, and that it's only by people working together (and that includes parents being sensible about the problems involved) that the problem will be solved.

It is honest and open attitudes on the part of parents, it is that vital communication factor, that leads young people to weigh the drugs scene up for themselves and reject it. It is our attitude of common sense and honesty that gives them the courage to 'just say no'. Saying no to pushers is the only way the problem will be solved. As in many other areas of life, prevention is better than cure.

Use your own family style when you want to discuss certain things that worry you with your teenager. Let's take cigarette smoking. There's no way you can stop a teenager from smoking if he or she is absolutely determined to smoke. Your son or daughter could smoke on the way to school, in the disco, in the pub, or when he or she is with friends. It's silly to say things like, 'Don't you ever let me catch you smoking.'

What you can do (and pick an approach to suit you) is to have a family discussion about smoking. Just point out that smoking brings in £4 billion each year to the government. It also kills 100,000 people each year. Lots of people do smoke (one-third of the adult population), but many of them wish they didn't. Most of them are sorry they took up the habit. It's easy to start smoking; it's very difficult to stop. The best thing is never to start.

All this is true and, whether you smoke or not, it remains true. If you do smoke you could say, 'I regret the day I started.' Say what you think. It doesn't have to be discussed formally. You can chat about it whilst you're out shopping with your teenager, when you've just had a visitor who smokes heavily, or just seen a programme on TV about smoking.

Your way of talking about the subject is crucial. Don't argue, talk about the subject. Don't dwell on horror stories about people who've died of lung cancer. If you smoke, don't deny that smoking does you harm. Be honest: it makes you cough, makes you short of breath and is a dirty, smelly habit. Admit it. Talk about the subject quietly and rationally and say what you really think. You could say something like: 'Anyone who smokes is a mug.'

That's your view. Now listen to what your son or daughter has to say about the subject. See what his or her attitude is. Don't argue or be too vehement; just listen. If you over-react (or, of course, threaten and issue dire warnings), you could make a problem where there wasn't one in the first place. Don't assume your teenager *is* going to smoke. Just chat about it and try to get across what a daft sort of pastime it is.

Alcohol, like cigarettes, is another addictive habit. Most drug addicts are addicted to cigarettes, alcohol and tranquillisers rather than pot or heroin. There are people who never drink at all; people who have a glass of something on special occasions, a party, or at Christmas; there are those who are social drinkers, who like a drink at home watching

TV, or like going to the pub for a drink; there are those who drink every day; and there are those who cannot live their lives without drink. It's estimated that one person in a hundred in our society falls within this last category. Alcoholism is a disease and it kills many thousands of people each year. Alcohol is the cause of thousands of deaths on the road; it is a major causal factor in the majority of cases of child abuse.

What do parents do about alcohol? You'll probably like a drink yourself (most parents do), but how do you get across to your teenager that alcohol can become a way of life, that it does involve risks of dependency, that it can, if taken in excess, severely damage the body? You may remember your first drink as a teenager, getting drunk on one or two pints of beer or a couple of glasses of spirits. Alcohol may make us do things we regret afterwards. It, like any other drug, gives us a temporary lift. It does nothing to solve our problems and adds nothing to the dignity of human life.

Many teenagers do drink. At the teenage parties my children had at home I was astonished by the sheer amount of alcohol consumed by both teenage boys and girls. For some teenagers, alcohol is a way of life. Some have become virtual alcoholics, and these will need help and support to kick the habit. If somebody in your family is a heavy drinker, there are organisations that can help you with the problem. Addresses are given at the back of the book.

What about the rest of the teenagers? You may think your son or daughter is too young to drink, or you may not want him or her to visit a pub or go to parties where a lot of drink is consumed and empty beer cans and wine bottles litter the floor. How do you get your teenager to choose not to drink, or at least to drink in a moderate, sensible way?

You can, as with cigarettes, discuss it calmly and sensibly. You can point out the cost, the fact that one can say 'no' to having a drink. Then I think you have to be positive and try to get your youngster to consider leisure activities which are active, not passive (and which don't rely on alcohol for providing enjoyment). Watching TV or sitting in a pub drinking are not the only choices teenagers have for passing the time. There are masses of leisure activities which are fun, rewarding and don't involve alcohol.

If your youngster takes up a sport and takes an interest in his or her body (perhaps attending weightlifting classes or a gymnasium), he or she is less likely to abuse the body with alcohol. Perhaps you could get your teenager to join the Youth Hostels Association or join the local youth club (your local reference library will have the address, together with lists of other activities for young people in your area). I am convinced that a great many youngsters drink out of boredom. They want danger, excitement, a 'buzz'. They resort to drinking to give them that feeling of danger and excitement.

If we want to stop teenagers drinking we have to provide danger, challenge and excitement in other ways. I asked one teenager recently why he drank so much.

'What else is there to do?' he answered.

That's a strange thing to say if you think about it. He was 18. Was there no sport that interested him? Fishing? Mountain climbing? Football? I asked him if he had any hobbies. 'No,' he said. He had been educated to be passive: to believe that he didn't need to do anything himself and that the State (or 'Them') was responsible for him.

How sad. You have to tell your youngster loud and clear that he or she is responsible for what happens in his or her life. There are plenty of causes your youngster can become involved in, political or social. There are people who are far worse off than us, who need our help. There are hundreds of human endeavours that a youngster can become involved in that will give him or her a feeling of pride, achievement and belonging. To do something useful with or for others, to take up a new hobby or interest, to join a new group or a political party is better than resorting to alcohol for kicks.

VANDALISM

It's the same with vandalism and football hooliganism. Young people resort to vandalism because they want to make their mark, to count, to be somebody. What you must do, as a parent, is to suggest ways in which they might be able to make their mark without resorting to an aerosol can. There are clubs, groups, classes they can join. They don't have to resort to violence and vandalism to get their kicks. Frustration leads to aggression. We as parents have to think of ways in which they can achieve, use their energies and feel more self-respect and respect for others.

To you it may seem incomprehensible that young people could go to a football match with the express purpose of causing trouble or fighting with the opposing supporters. Why do they do it? If you ask them the answer is: 'Excitement, innit? Those players are my heroes. What good is it having heroes if you don't support them?' What the rest of us do is pay attention to football supporters when they behave badly (newspaper coverage, reports on TV). We ignore them when they behave well. This is one of the most effective ways of encouraging anti-social behaviour.

All you can do with your youngster, if he or she is a football fanatic and goes to the local game, is to go with him or her. You could forbid your youngster to go if you're afraid of crowd violence (or let him or her go with an adult, or sit in the stands). Better still, you could divert your youngster's need for excitement into *playing* football, or rugby, or taking up some other sport such as motorbike scrambling or cycle racing. It's a comment on all of us that we can't provide better ways for our young people to find danger and excitement than to inflict violence on other people at football matches.

Boredom and frustration lead to aggression or depression. With young teenagers it's essential to get over that the solution to boredom lies in their hands. Parents (or the State) can't do everything for them. They need adventure, but some of the time they have to say, 'I'm going to get off my bottom and *do* something rather than just sitting here.' Even in economically depressed areas there are always groups to be joined, people to be helped, interests and hobbies that don't cost a lot of money. Parents have to stress that it's being active, not passive, that solves problems, gets things done and imparts self-respect.

Few of us are heroes to our own teenagers, but teenagers need heroes and heroines, somebody to look up to, admire, identify with. Those heroes and heroines don't have to be pop stars, footballers, film stars. They can be the man or woman in the youth club down the road, or a political leader, or somebody who does practical work to help other people. That's why I don't think teenagers should spend too much time watching TV. They need real heroes, not fictional ones, and those heroes are to be found in the community out there, being active and not letting life pass them by, or resorting to non-loving sex or drugs to provide the fizz and excitement in their lives.

What is the best way that you, as a parent, can go about giving your teenager this positive attitude to life, so that his or her life is active and not passive? I think you should:

- *Be positive yourself.*
  Be active yourself in the community. Set a good example. If you sit slumped in front of the telly every evening, if you have no interests or hobbies yourself, you are suggesting a passive, defeatist attitude towards the world and its woes.

- *Encourage.*
  Say, 'You can do it.' Don't put your youngster down. (Who needs that?) Get him or her to take an active interest in community matters and get him or her to *join* things. Boredom is Public Enemy Number One as far as teenagers are concerned.

- *Show affection to your teenager.*
  What's the point of loving your teenager if you never show it? Often, involvement with sex, drugs and anti-social behaviour is a symptom of the fact that the young person's need for love and affection is not being met. Don't treat words of affection as though they were £20 notes. Do say, 'I love you' to your teenager sometime. It's true, so say it.

● *Don't dominate, warn, threaten.*
Make a few common-sense statements about casual sex, drugs, vandalism, football hooliganism, and then listen to what your teenager has to say. His or her opinions have value too. Discuss options, choices. Let your youngster come to a decision. Trust him or her to act sensibly. Trust works better than suspicion or bombast.

● *Don't dodge issues.*
Give your teenager the facts, if you know them. Give an honest, sincere answer when he or she asks a question. It's the attitude that's vital, not the answer.

● *Seek help when you need it.*
Your local Citizens' Advice Bureau will provide help that is free and confidential, and tell you where to go to find the help you need. Getting the right kind of help for your teenager can save months of worry and distress.

● *Have faith in your teenager.*
Discuss issues with your youngster as you would with a friend: openly, honestly and sincerely. Then leave it to her or him to choose to do the right thing. Most do. Most steer a path through the moral wasteland that surrounds. Give your teenager credit for that. Remember you're not perfect yourself, but who needs perfect parents? A teenager will settle for honesty.

● *Care.*
Teenagers are exploited and many of them are led to unreal expectations and a feeling that everybody else is doing better than they are. Sympathise. Don't say: 'I can't do anything with him or her.' Keep the channels of communication open. Say something about your own worries and frustrations. Tell your teenager how it is for you and he or she will tell you how it is for him or her. That's honesty and real communication.

7

Teenagers who can't find work

You go to a party and chat to someone you've never met before. The chances are that, sooner or later, he or she will ask you: 'What do you do?' That means, in other words, 'What is your job?'

I don't like the question. When I tell people I'm a psychologist they tend to ask me, 'Can you read my mind?' The truth is, I don't want to (it's rather like asking a dentist to have a quick look at your teeth). I can understand, though, why people are interested in what other people do, what their job is. Our work is a large part of our identity.

Work is terribly important to all of us. It gives us an opportunity to belong to a group, to make new friends and acquaintances. Work gives us status, belonging, a role in society. It gives us a daily programme of activity, a reason for living. It gives us dignity, it imposes a discipline on our lives and it provides us with money.

It's a mistake, in my view, to think that work is solely to do with money. I once met a man who had been left half-a-million pounds by a maiden aunt. *He still worked.*

'I'm a prep school teacher,' he told me. 'I like teaching.'

He could have lived in Bermuda or Majorca, sat around all day and done nothing. He chose to work. Perhaps, after a few weeks, sitting around all day doing nothing loses its appeal. Perhaps work provided him with some of the things I've mentioned.

There *are* rich people who do no work, just as there are plenty who do work but not for financial reasons. Money does enable people to handle the problem of leisure more effectively. Most unemployed people aren't rich. They have time for everything and money for nothing. It's hard to cope with too much leisure when you are stoney broke.

There's another problem. Most of us are affected by the Calvinist work ethic (God favours those who work hard. The devil finds work for idle hands to do). Many of us feel guilty when we don't work. We feel a sense of shame, of failure. Work is very closely bound up with self-respect. Not to work can rob us of our self-esteem.

In our work-orientated society, what you do is what you are. Or is it? What if you don't? What if, through no fault of your own, you don't have a job? Do you still exist as a person? Clearly you do. You still have a need to affirm your personality, a chance to make your mark on the world, an opportunity to belong.

When a man loses his job, it affects him as a person. The loss of a job may radically affect the whole family. When you throw the stone of unemployment into the family pond, the ripples wash over everybody: father, mother and children alike. There are lots of people, men and women, who are jobless, at home all day, no longer part of the community and no longer feeling that they belong.

Many teenagers (sincere, bright, willing to work) can't find jobs. Some of them feel depressed. Some of them suffer from 'dole sickness', a sad mixture of shame, lethargy and hopelessness. Ten or twenty years ago most of them would have found jobs. Now, because of changes in work patterns (and world-wide economic recession) many of them can't find jobs. What can you as a parent do to help them?

First, you have to understand what's happening in the world and what changes are taking place in our society. Oil price increases in 1973 and 1979 resulted in a depressed world economy and the most severe output recession of this century. Coupled with this was an information technology revolution which brought technology into every industrial and commercial activity, and which meant that many jobs which had previously been done by people were now being done by machines.

The theme of the last 10 to 15 years has been *change*. What we have seen in Britain is the decline of heavy industry and a move towards the post-industrial society. There has been a continual shift from production industries (such as ship-building, steel, engineering and construction) towards service industries (finance, business services, leisure, transport and communications, computer technology). This change has taken place on a nationwide basis.

You will have gained your overall picture of unemployment from television or newspapers. You will know that there are millions of people unemployed, you will know of people who have lost their jobs (you may have lost your own job), and you will have seen factories closing down and know about the devastation in the heart of once-great industrial cities.

I know about this myself. I've visited northern cities and spoken to some of the unemployed youngsters living there. In one city, speaking to some teenagers working on an urban farm project, I asked one of them, 'What do you think of the work?' He replied, 'Not much. What I'd like is a proper job, in a factory, like my dad used to have.' I understood what he meant, but I couldn't help feeling that the 'proper job' he refers to might well have disappeared.

I'm not telling this story to spread gloom and despondency; we have enough of that already. I'm telling it because we must all, parents and teenagers, start thinking of new jobs, different patterns of work, different opportunities, and these opportunities will vary from area to area. There may be jobs or opportunities for training available in your area if you know where to look, so encourage your youngster to be positive and persistent in his or her search for work. Young people *need* to work. Work provides them with self-respect, a daily time-table, a purpose in their lives.

In school, young people will have been taught the 'three Rs' (reading, writing and arithmetic). Parents have to encourage in their teenagers when they leave school the 'three Ss' (self-reliance, self-starting, i.e. initiative, and self-respect). More and more employers are looking for young people with personal qualities, for response-ability, for the ability to get on with other people. That's why it's no use moaning, grumbling, blaming, if a young person can't find a job. A little bit of praise and encouragement is much more helpful to him or her than constant criticism.

- *Be practical.*
  Find out whether there are any small firms setting up in
  your area who will need employees. (By 1990, small firms
  are expected to increase their workforce by about 700,000
  people, many of them full time.) What are the opportunities for self-employment? Are there any part-time
  jobs (in hotels, pubs, restaurants, offices, at the local
  hospital)? What opportunities are there for training?

- *Gain all the information you can.*
  Arrange an interview with your local Careers Officer and
  make sure your youngster goes along to find out what
  jobs or training schemes are available in your area. (The
  number of your local Careers Service is in the telephone
  book, or the operator will give it to you). If there are no
  jobs, get details of training schemes.

- *Be positive.*
  A training scheme, you could argue, is not a 'proper job'.
  It can lead to a job, however. At the end of training the
  young people will be helped to find work if they haven't
  found a job by then. Doing something gives the teenager
  self-respect. It teaches him or her social skills, life skills,
  self-discipline, how to get on with other people, how to
  use his or her initiative, how to get to work on time. In
  my view that's better than sitting at home all day
  becoming more and more depressed.
      Money is not the main criterion. On a training scheme
  a young person can mix with other young people, can
  share ideas, talk, discuss (and get out of the house).
  These interpersonal skills will be useful when or if he or
  she does find a job. The fact of doing *something* will also
  enhance your youngster's self-regarding sentiment.

- *Be helpful.*
  Show your youngster how to write a letter of application
  for a job. If you don't know your Careers Office will
  advise you. Show him or her how to fill in an application
  form for a job and how to use the telephone. You could

discuss the best way to dress for a particular interview, how to behave during the interview, and how to give the best possible impression of one's abilities. Again your Careers Office will give you advice on this. If your teenager applies for a job and fails to get it, say something like: 'You tried. You feel very down and disappointed. Never mind. Better luck next time.'

Your attitude does have a vital part to play in your youngster's reaction to unemployment. We know that unemployment is a terrible thing. It can lead to depression, illness and feelings of hopelessness. That's why you, as a parent, have to try hard to strike a positive note and look for every chance you can see of getting your youngster a full-time or part-time job. It doesn't help to blame or to criticise.

It may be that in the future we will create more jobs by the introduction of a shorter working week, earlier retirement, part-time work and the banning of overtime. Be that as it may, your youngster (and all of us) may have to learn that work is not necessarily a paid, full-time job. A part-time job may provide him or her with the community involvement needed, as may unpaid voluntary work, a sport, a hobby, or taking part in activities organised by the local youth service. A full-time job for which payment is received *isn't* essential to mental health. Contact with other people is.

This is why it really is essential to find out what is going on in your area. You may live in the city or in the country; wherever you live there will be unemployment, but there will also be schemes to help young people, there will be communal activities, youth clubs, training programmes, sports clubs and opportunities for voluntary work. It's important for you to know what's going on in your own locality. Your local reference library will give you the information you need.

Some young people have told me that they don't like training schemes. One 17-year-old told me that he thought that they were 'just cheap labour' and 'they don't get you anywhere'. I disagree. Many of the schemes do lead on to jobs. They prevent boredom and loneliness. They give the youngster some hope, a reason to get up in the morning. The alternative is hopelessness, cynicism, despair. Young people can suffer loss of social skills simply by getting out of the habit of meeting people by remaining isolated at home.

Work can be a grinding, back-breaking business. Some jobs are dirty and unpleasant, but people seem to humanise the situation, make it bearable. I'm not sure that people, adults and teenagers, can do without some sort of work, some sort of group. Prolonged unemployment is a profoundly distressing experience. It chips away at the soul, and at one's identity.

When I gave up my job and started out as a full-time writer, two things happened. My wife felt, so she's told me since, 'strange, odd, all wrong'. I stayed at home writing while the rest of the family went off to school or work. I was there when they came home in the evening.

It certainly felt strange to me. I missed talking to people at work, catching up on the lastest gossip or scandal, or just having a chat, talking about where people were going for their holidays. I looked forward to Tuesdays and Thursdays when a pal would call round and we'd go for a drink together. I was suffering from lack of human contact, from loneliness. If those were my feelings as an adult (and remember, I had my writing), I can imagine how isolated an unemployed teenager at home all day must feel.

Prevention is better than cure. I hope you will, as a parent, go to your youngster's school and find out all you can about the GCSE (General Certificate of Secondary Education) and what its aims are with regard to the pupils. Is your youngster being taught co-operation (how to work together in groups with other youngsters)? Is he or she being taught problem-solving as well as facts? Is he or she being taught how to think, how to analyse facts, how to communicate? These are vital skills for the future.

I hope you'll discuss with your youngster's careers master or mistress the jobs that are likely to be available in the future and what sort of skills will be needed in those jobs. The jobs may be in leisure or tourism, in personal services, in catering, computing or technology. The job situation changes from year to year and from area to area. You should find out what the situation is *before* your youngster leaves school.

I hope that you'll encourage your youngster's interests and hobbies, and remember that an interest (for example in computers, dressmaking, fashion, windsurfing, climbing, the countryside) might be the gateway to a job once he or she has left school. The days of 'blue chip' jobs are over. What counts now is real interests, flexibility, initiative and personality (those inter-personal skills I mentioned before).

If your teenager doesn't have a job, there may be youth centres or a drop-in centre locally where he or she can gain advice, support and information about local job initiatives. As in other areas of life, it doesn't help to pick up your youngster's despondency. Your job as a parent is to accentuate the positive and not let a mood of apathy and despair take over.

There's no doubt about the psychological harm that unemployment can cause young people. I've seen unemployed young people going to sign on with pink hair and wild hairstyles, but dressed in black, as though in mourning. I've seen youngsters clinging to enormous transistor radios (the boys wearing leather lace-up boots) as though all that noise and racket was something they needed now that factories and great shipyards are no more. The industrial age is gone. The era of the micro chip is now with us. The teenagers of today are youngsters of an age of great transition. They are in at the birth of the post-industrial society, and it's not an easy time for any of us. It demands new ideas, new attitudes, new ways of looking at the whole concept of work.

The Calvinist work ethic provided a solution to the problem of leisure and free time by ensuring that there was very little leisure available. My own father worked six days a week, worked in his garden on Sunday, and had one week's holiday every year. He didn't have to worry about what to do in his spare time. He didn't have any.

Faced with unemployment, young people and adults have to face up to the problem of diversion: how to spend the day that looms before them. More and more of us will, in the years to come, be faced with the problem of what to do with our leisure, as we work shorter hours, retire earlier, work part-time or are unemployed.

It may be that in the twenty-first century what you are will not be what you do but what your leisure interests are. There is no absolute necessity for a job to define an individual. What we may learn to take into account is not the person's job but his or her personal interests, his or her hobbies, talents, community involvements. Some young people are learning not to feel guilty about being unemployed. Is that a good thing or not?

Parents have told me, 'My daughter's a lazy good-for-nothing. All she does is sit about all day or go out with her friends. She's not interested in finding a job;' or, 'My son's driving me mad. He gets up at 1 pm. Then he watches television. Then he goes out with his mates. What kind of a life is that?' It's a life on the dole. These young people assess each other not by what they do but by what they are. Perhaps we ought to start learning from them that a full-time, paid job is not the sole source of our identity.

It isn't easy for us to learn that lesson. In our society today, the protestant work ethic still operates since we know more about work than we do about leisure and are more practised, most of us, at working than we are at making use of long periods of free time. Jobs are still accorded status. (A house-wife scores 1, a mother 3, a fashion designer 10 and a brain surgeon 10.) We don't ask what qualities of character the brain surgeon has. We grant him or her respect simply because of his or her high-status profession.

We can't do that with unemployed youngsters: they don't have a job or profession. So how can we boost their self-respect, given the fact that they are lacking the status and sense of achievement that having a 'proper job' bestows? I think parents should ask their teenagers how they feel about their situation. Parents with unemployed teenagers should:

- *Have some sympathy with them.*
  Realise that they are entitled to their benefit cheques from social security and don't say things like, 'In my day we never took money for doing nothing. We had to work for

it.' That's an entirely negative comment and does nothing to boost their self-respect.

- *Listen to them.*
  Listen to what they have to say about their frustration when they go down to the Job Centre and can't find a job. That's bad enough; it's not fair to lower their self-esteem further with sarcastic or critical comments.

- *Discuss facts.*
  It isn't the fault of teenagers that they haven't got a job. Find out about unpaid work such as looking after children, keeping old people company, helping the handicapped. The local Citizens' Advice Bureau or your local youth club will advise you.

- *Look at the local paper and find out what part-time and casual jobs are available,*
  such as delivering leaflets, being a waiter or waitress, cleaning, gardening, window cleaning, bar work (for youngsters over 18) or part-time work in a shop or large department store. There may also be seasonal work available such as farm work, hotel work, Christmas work in shops or helping with the post.

- *Make sure teenagers know about the benefits they are entitled to.*
  These may include unemployment benefit, supplementary benefit, free dental treatment, glasses, prescriptions or special payments such as money to buy a winter coat or a suit for an interview. (The Careers Office will advise you on benefits.)

- *Encourage.*
  Tell teenagers to keep their ears to the ground, that quite a few people get jobs by hearing about them informally. Encourage part-time work because it develops interpersonal skills and adds to youngsters' experience. Get your youngsters organised in writing letters, filling in forms and phoning with regard to jobs. A word of

practical advice is worth 10 speeches about how idle teenagers are or what the world was like in 1960.

- *If you are unemployed yourself as a parent try not to pass on your own despondency and depression to your youngsters.*
  What they need is hope and encouragement. Do try to take up a hobby, sport or interest to get you out of the house so that you are not constantly in each other's company (and getting on each other's nerves).

We know that unemployment is stressful. It brings poverty and stress trailing along in its wake; it is a severe blow to a young person's self-regard. However, not all young people sink into apathy or despair through unemployment. Some do motivate themselves into action, and action – doing something – is always less stressful than sitting at home doing nothing and worrying, sinking into a pit of listlessness, anger or depression.

What I would like to suggest is a self-help programme for young people who leave school and find themselves without a job. Let's return to those 'three S's' (self-reliance, self-starting, self-respect) and see what the vital elements are in such a programme. The aim is to prevent teenagers from sinking into the apathy syndrome and losing their pride and confidence in themselves.

Self-reliance

When your youngster leaves school, encourage him or her to look for a job straight away, to go for different interviews, send off application forms and be determined about trying to get a job.

Encourage him or her not to settle for life on the dole but to say: 'I'm going to *do* something, anything, rather than sit at home brooding.' If no job is available, do encourage your youngster to join a training scheme. This is specific skill training and can lead to vocational qualifications.

If your youngster is sceptical about training schemes, tell

him or her that there are plenty of young people who have gained work experience and have gone on to get a job or to start off a small business. These are the sorts of areas in which your teenager might be able to convert work experience into a proper job: building, car maintenance, dress-making and fashion, computers, upholstery, catering. I know young people who now have their own businesses, having accrued the relevant experience after leaving school and gained as much knowledge as they could in their particular field.

These businesses include house repairs and maintenance, a small garage, the making and selling of evening dresses, a secondhand thirties fashions boutique, a small computer games company, an upholstery and furniture repair business, a sandwich bar.

The vital factor to remember is that it may be possible to survive on social security payments but a job or a place on a training scheme gives hope for the future and encourages a pattern whereby the young person can impose some discipline and structure on his or her life, as well as developing skills and interests which may lead on to a job in the future.

This attitude, plus a degree of community involvement (knowing what is available in the way of recreation and support for young people in the area), means that your youngster is adopting an active, not a passive, attitude to unemployment. Being active and self-reliant, trying for jobs and not being easily discouraged, will pay off in the long run. The alternative is to be lonely, isolated and miserable.

Self-starting

Your youngster should try to impose a daily routine on the day. He or she should get up at a regular time, wash his or her hair regularly, try to keep a reasonably attractive appearance, try to keep fit (by going on a morning run, taking up weightlifting or going along to a multi-gym or sports club).

If this sounds too much like preparation for the next Olympic games, modify it, but have a routine which gives a shape and pattern to the day. Go to the Job Centre on a particular day. On another day, see if any help is needed at the local market or any other place where there's something going on that involves mixing with and talking to a variety of people. To stay home all day is a very debilitating experience and does nothing to boost a young person's self-image.

Encourage any artistic or practical gifts your youngster may have. Knitted sweaters, greetings cards, crocheted hats, hand made jewellery can all be sold; items bought at a jumble sale can perhaps be re-sold at a profit. Helping friends to maintain cars or motorbikes or giving a hand with house maintenance all entail the learning of skills which may come in useful at a later date.

There are other unemployed youngsters who are also wanting to do something with the day. Why not start up a fringe theatre group (and perhaps give shows to local schools or the local senior citizens)? Start an animal sanctuary or set up a club where local young people can come on a certain day to pursue their hobbies and interests. Get local businessmen and women to support the venture. This involvement with the community, and taking the initiative in starting up new ventures, is the best way to shake off apathy and fatalism.

Young people have to learn to say: 'I can do something, and I'm going to do it. I'm fed up hanging about waiting for something to happen. I'm going to make it happen.' That's a far more healthy attitude than saying, 'What's the use?' Take an interest and develop that interest within a group. Start up a netball team, a swimming club, an animal welfare group. Community feeling and working alongside others to achieve something are the best antidotes to neurosis and despair.

What about money? It's important, but less vital than self-respect. If your youngster helps out in a restaurant, or does odd jobs for people, or becomes involved with helping the handicapped or old people, it's the involvement with the world of work and with the community that's so important. That leads on to self-respect, to more show of initiative and to self-confidence. It is contact with other people, not money, which is vital to mental health.

Self-respect

You must encourage your youngster to be active and persistent in his or her efforts to get a job. You must tell him or her that it *is* a difficult time for young people to live in and that you respect your youngster for his or her attempts to cope with the world.

Your youngster will gain self-respect from what you say in response to his or her efforts to find a job. Be brisk, sensible and encouraging. Say: 'You're really trying hard to find something, and I respect you for that.' Praise is vital, so do show appreciation when your youngster does make an effort to beat the trap of apathy and despair which unemployment can lead to.

Your youngster will find self-respect in achievements. Encourage him or her to impose self-control and discipline on his or her life. Tell your teenager that it is better to join a training scheme or a work-initiative programme than to sit at home all day. Praise those efforts that he or she does make to impose a *raison d'être* and a structure on his or her life and don't adopt a complaining, critical attitude towards your youngster. Young people *want* to do something worthwhile. Your job is to encourage your teenager in this direction and to tell him or her that he or she can find something to do and a purpose in life if he or she tries hard and refuses to give in to scepticism and apathy.

The most impressive example of a programme of self-help that I have ever come across concerned a woman I read about in the *Reader's Digest* some years ago. She was interned in a Japanese prisoner-of-war camp and was locked for most of the day in a tiny prison cell.

What the woman did was to think of all the cities of the world she would like to visit, including Vienna, Berlin, Rome, New York, Venice, Florence and Madrid. She then worked out how far it was from her prison cell to each city and measured the distance across her cell.

Each day she walked and, over three years, walked thousands of miles 'visiting' each city. At the end of the war she was freed from her prison and she really did go to all of those cities that she'd 'visited' one by one in her tiny prison cell.

I tell that story because I think it says something about human courage, initiative and determination to survive. I have no illusions about unemployment or about the great pain and mental distress that changing from an industrial to a technological society brings to tens of thousands of human beings in our country.

There is no easy answer to unemployment. The world is going through a period of great economic and industrial change. Britain once dominated world markets. Now, other countries can produce goods cheaper and export to Britain many products which we once manufactured ourselves and exported abroad.

The economic outlook sometimes looks bleak and depressing, but we are a nation of innovators. We no longer rule an empire, but we do have vast human resources and people who are adaptable, inventive and energetic. My view is that we will adapt to these changes, find ways of facing up to new modes of living, new technologies, new ideas, new lifestyles. This is an age of transition from the old to the new. We know what the old was like; I think we are in the painful process of creating the new, and that new life can give us all more leisure, more dignity, more humanity. It can give young people a fulfilling life and hope for the future.

In that new way of life, a full-time paid job will not be the only criterion by which we judge a human being. We'll learn to judge a person by what he or she *is* rather than by what he or she does, by what that person contributes to the community and the involvement that the person has in the welfare and care of others. The post-industrial society could be a much more humane world for us all.

What we are seeing all around us now are the first, painful birth pangs of a new way of life, in which people and community will be paramount, and personal qualities, social commitment and caring for others will come to the fore. We'll still need to be inventive and energetic to produce the wealth to sustain that more caring society. I think we'll do it. I think we'll respond to change and solve the problems of the present and the future. I have great faith in the courage and adaptability of the young people who have to face up to these great challenges which confront them.

What can you as a parent do to help your youngster in these times of transition and unemployment? I think you should:

- *Liaise with your youngster's school whilst he or she is still there and get all the careers advice you can.*
  Nowadays there are thousands of new careers and new skills which parents and teenagers need to be told about, as they need to be informed as to which skills are likely to be in demand in the future.

- *If your teenager leaves school without a job, find out all you can about training and other job initiatives in your area.*
  Don't let your youngster develop apathetic attitudes and lie in bed all day. Do encourage him or her to gain experience and skills which may lead on to work (whether it be self-employed or paid full-time or part-time) in the future.

- *Discuss the situation with your youngster and listen to what he or she has to say.*
  Show some sympathy and understanding of the situation your youngster is in. Don't start off your contribution to the discussion by saying, 'In my day . . .' Those days are over. These are new problems and they'll only be solved by courage, initiative and by parents who encourage their youngster to talk about his or her feelings, who listen to what the teenager's views are, and constantly praise and genuinely respect any initiative the youngster shows in his or her attempts to overcome the depressing effects of being unemployed.

- *Explain that training schemes and other work initiatives are not primarily about getting more money.*
  They are about gaining confidence, social contact and social skills, as well as learning a vocational skill that

could lead on to a job. It gives the youngster an idea of what work is and helps him or her to develop inter-personal skills. This, in my view, is better than saying, 'I'll settle for the dole.'

- *Be positive.*
  In your area the employment situation may be very bleak. It doesn't help your youngster if you are depressed, pessimistic or apathetic. There's always something to do in the community; there are other people to work together with; there are projects to be started, goals to be achieved. Do be optimistic, hopeful and encouraging (and don't forget to listen to what your youngster has to say).

Unemployment is a debilitating, depressing experience, but it can be tackled given energy, persistence, guts, courage, determination and initiative. It's a fearsome dragon but it can be slain so do pass on a message of hope to your youngster. Get him or her to say, 'I'll give it a try,' rather than to say, 'Why bother?' Not to bother, not to try is defeatist, so do tell your teenager, 'You'll win, you'll find a job eventually.' That's a good, positive message to get across.

8
The problem page

If I had my way I'd set up Parent of Teenager Support Groups (PTSGs) throughout the land. These would be the equivalent of playgroups or Mother-and-Toddler groups but they would be for the mothers and fathers of teenage children.

Why would I do it? Simply because parents of teenagers need support in bringing up their children. When you have a problem, you can solve it yourself or call in an expert to help you to solve it. (A list of addresses, useful if you're facing a crisis with your youngster, is given at the back of this book.)

Sometimes, though, you can't solve it yourself and you don't want to call in a psychologist. What you want to do is to talk to other parents about it. That's when you find out that you're not the only parent who's ever faced the problem, that you're not a failure, that plenty of other parents have that problem too, and that there are ways of dealing with it that you may not have thought of.

RIVALRY

Let's take an example. Several years ago a distraught mum came up to me and said: 'My two teenage girls fight like cat and dog. They're always borrowing each other's clothes, always fighting and arguing over everything. They don't seem to like each other at all. Is this kind of thing normal?'

Then, I had teenagers of my own. 'Believe me,' I told her, 'it's very normal indeed.'

I told the mother about my daughter who, as an infant, used to spit in her brother's pram: a graphic enough expression of her feelings towards him. I told her about a friend of mine who, when I mentioned my daughter's behaviour to her, said: 'That's nothing. When I was a baby my brother set fire to my pram *with me in it.*'

A certain amount of rivalry between siblings is very common. The psychologist Alfred Adler considered it to be an important aspect of a child's development. He confessed that the whole of his life he strove to outdo his elder brother. I think it's very sad when dislike of, or competition with, a sibling lasts a lifetime (which of course it can).

What is more common is for a child or teenager to go through a stage where he or she intensely dislikes a particular brother or sister. The two may grow very close to each other as adults, especially when they have homes and families of their own. Sometimes, siblings who have been very close as children drift apart in later life. What we're usually dealing with, as far as teenage rivalry is concerned, is a particular age and stage and a particular situation.

Take that mother. What I advised her to do was to make her two teenagers responsible for washing and ironing their own clothes. (They were 16 and 17. They had a washing machine in the house.) This would save arguments every week over whose bra was whose and would say to the teenagers: 'Take the responsibility for that chore.'

Next each was to keep her clothes quite separate from the other's. Neither was to borrow any item of clothing without permission. That was to be a firm rule. If any arguments broke out, the mother was to say immediately to them: 'I'm not having this. Susan (the eldest daughter), go upstairs and stay there until I tell you you can come down.' Mother was to show that she was really angry over the squabbling, and not say (as she had previously): 'Oh, you two, do stop arguing.'

Mother was to tell the two girls about 'yours' and 'mine', that there are certain things that belong to people and they don't like those things interfered with, looked at, rootled through or borrowed by others. Lastly, she was to say to them: 'I'm not having any more arguments.' She was to be attentive to the girls if they didn't argue, and do little things for them but not wash their clothes. She was to be unpleasant and silent towards them if they argued.

The mother told me a month later that the arguments had

ceased. What she'd done in fact was make it obvious what she wanted, allocated clear responsibility to each of them, and stopped paying attention to them (and so rewarding them) when they argued. Squabbles and arguments, as attention-seeking devices, can work like a charm. They cease to work when one arguer is sent elsewhere, the other is diverted to doing something, and the parent makes it quite clear that she or he is not going to put up with that behaviour.

Clearly, this doesn't sort out the problem of sibling rivalry in general (and the two could still argue when you're not there). The rules for dealing with sibling rivalry are as follows:

- *Give everybody a role in the family.*

- *Don't let your children manipulate you.*
  If they do, it could last a lifetime. Make it clear that you won't put up with it, that you have some rights as well.

- *Don't treat each teenager the same.*
  Each one is quite different, so draw out the best from each and don't be forever comparing one to the detriment of another.

- *Give your children jobs to do separately, but let them see that life is about co-operation as well as competition.*
  After six months, the two girls I mentioned started to take weekly turns in doing the washing (no squabbles). It was simply quicker that way. I often swapped my Day of Hell with one of my teenagers, or we helped each other when one of us was pushed. Clear guidelines as to who does what save squabbles and make co-operation more likely, not less.

- *If war breaks out or petty squabbles begin, don't join in (and certainly don't take sides).*
  Just say, 'I'm not having this.' Turn the TV off (if it's on) and send the oldest teenager to his or her bedroom. They'll soon see the sense of peace treaties rather than arguments.

- *Get your teenagers to join different clubs, take up different interests.*
  Do some things together as a family, but always emphasise that each youngster has something special to contribute (i.e. what he or she can do and what he or she is). Never say things like, 'I wish you were more like Shirley.' She *isn't* Shirley. Say, 'What I like about you is . . .' That's positive and to do with that youngster's uniqueness.

- *You may love one child more than another.*
  So what? You can still treat them fairly, not have a pet – or a family scapegoat. Children and teenagers don't want to be loved equally: they want to be treated fairly and loved for themselves.

Giving support to the teenager in a way that suits his or her own temperament is an important principle. One youngster may need a lot of overt affection, another may be embarrassed by it. An occasional hand on the arm or arm around the shoulder may be sufficient to show your love. Teenagers are not the same, even within the same family, and we need to show that we understand their individual needs.

Consider jealousy between teenagers. It occurs in the best-regulated households. Somebody's got something we want, whether it's a special talent, good looks or a new pair of shoes. We feel jealous. Fear is a part of jealousy. We fear that someone may take away something or someone we love. Jealousy is a very powerful emotion. It can destroy affection, distort our perception of the world, make us do things which are unworthy of us.

The answer to jealousy is self-respect and, as in the case of sibling rivalry, which may be more ongoing than jealousy, the answer is to build up your teenager's self-regarding sentiment so that he or she doesn't feel the need to be jealous. You do that by:

- *Not comparing.*
  We all have to learn to set the bar of personal achievement at a height to suit ourselves. I don't compare myself with Shakespeare, or other writers. I just do my best. You

mustn't compare yourself with that super-efficient mum or dad up the road, and you must not compare one of your youngsters with another. They're *individuals*.

- *Not having favourites.*
  If you have one teenager who can do no wrong and one who's wrong all the time (i.e. the scapegoat in the family, the one who gets the blame), it's simply unfair, unjust. Be fair. Think of your family as a small repertory theatre and give everybody a chance to be a star. Give everybody a part and swap those parts around. Don't have one teenager playing the villain all of the time.

- *Not dishing out love and compliments as though they were £50 notes.*
  Be generous. Praise the one you like, feel close to them, but don't forget to say something nice to the one you've 'gone off' for a while. If an older teenager has more privileges, don't forget to give the younger one some special treats too (and make sure that the older one has more responsibilities in the home). Love isn't water in a bucket it's a mighty ocean, so don't be stingey with it.

If you follow these rules you'll still get some jealousy among your teenagers. Of course you will; it's inevitable. Life *isn't* fair. But you can try to be fair and be aware that one is doing badly, feeling low, whilst the other is doing well. This is a very good test of parental sensitivity.

Take that younger one, or the one who's feeling jealous, demoralised, to one side. Say: 'You're very special to me, you know.' Say some of the things you value in that teenager. Do this at a quiet time when he or she can have your undivided attention. Little words of understanding, of praise once a week, a month, mean so much to the youngster who is going through a jealous patch. They are all special, so do give each one the Good Treatment from time to time.

None of us has any need to be jealous if we're doing our best at what we're good at and feel that we're being appreciated for our efforts. It's awful to be in a race that you know you'll lose before you start. It isn't a race in a family; it's not a competition. Each member of the family is unique, so give everybody a special place in your heart. That, plus being fair, is the way to avoid jealousy.

What happens, though, if you feel that you dislike a youngster intensely, or you don't get on at all? You can't love all your youngsters the same, but you can have a sense of justice. What is it about the teenager that you don't like? Is it something that reminds you of something within you? Did you want a boy and were disappointed the child was a girl? (Or the other way around.) Does the child simply irritate you the whole time?

Be fair. Try to treat the teenager in a way that gives him or her some responsibility and prestige. If you think that you can expect nothing from him or her, a self-fulfilling prophecy will set in and nothing is what you'll get. If the teenager irritates you, keep your distance, have boundaries. Encourage your youngster to help out at an old people's home or with the handicapped. Let him or her take up an activity which will get him or her out of the house so you won't be under each other's feet the whole time. A little absence makes the heart grow fonder.

We all go through stages where we 'go off' a particular teenager. We may go through a stage where we don't like a teenager at all. Many's the mother or father who's told me, 'I like him now he's older. When he was a teenager we didn't get on at all.' (They've said the same thing about teenage daughters.) We have to remember that nobody's perfect, including you and me. We all need breaks from each other, we do get on each other's nerves from time to time, but if we hang in there, being as fair as we can, that teenager that we disliked so much can become a very good and close friend in later life.

Try to keep the channels of communication open. Say: 'I love you but I don't like the way you're behaving towards me.' Don't expect perfection and remember that you have faults as well. After all, there are loads of articles in magazines written about difficult teenagers. There are very few written about difficult parents! Give each other a break, don't keep getting on to one another, and keep your fingers crossed! I'll guarantee that you'll like each other more when the youngster leaves home. You'll see less of each other and begin to appreciate each more as real people and not just mirror images of your worst faults.

Let's turn now to shyness. What can you do about it if you have a very shy teenager, and should you do anything about it? A father once wrote to me after reading an article I'd written on shyness: 'Please leave shy people alone. There's nothing wrong with being shy.'

I agree. If your youngster is shy and contented, and can join in with others when the situation demands, then leave well alone. Some people are born shy, it's their nature to be shy, and I'm not suggesting that we try to turn shy youngsters into raving extroverts. That's wrong. It's like trying to change a piano into a violin.

On the other hand, if your youngster seems lonely and if his or her shyness brings isolation and unhappiness, then I think you ought to do something about it. What can you do? You can remember the importance of self-respect, a theme which runs through this book, and use PPR (see p. 18) to build up his or her confidence. You can look out for any special interests or skills your youngster has and encourage him or her in this direction.

Anything will do. It can be baking a cake, skateboarding, weaving, knitting, wind-surfing, amateur dramatics, car mechanics, woodwork. If your teenager enjoys it, and if it gives him or her a chance to meet other people, then do be supportive and say, 'Go for it.' The way we gain status in a group is to be good at something, and it can be anything from astronomy to swimming as long as it gives us an interest, a role and some status amongst our peers.

If you're shy yourself, discuss shyness with your youngster. Say it's OK to be shy and to admit to others that you're shy. Say that, if your youngster does join an after-school society or a youth club, or the guides or scouts, the first evening is always the worst. It's the first step which is so scarey for shy people. So assure your youngster you'll give him or her plenty of moral support and maybe take him or her along on that first occasion.

Criticism doesn't work with shy people and nor does forcing things, making comments like: 'Why haven't you got lots of friends like your sister?' That's very demoralising. There may be another shy youngster in the class you could introduce yours to. You could get your youngster to think of someone he or she would like to invite home to tea or go out with you on an outing.

Some tips for helping shy teenagers are:

● *Give them a job to do when you have visitors.*
It can be helping you to cook or just handing out crisps. Encourage them to do a job which will entail mingling with your guests. They'll find it's not as awful as it looks!

● *Let them help out at the local playgroup or help visiting elderly people.*
Many shy youngsters are marvellous with young children or the elderly.

● *Let them help at a local stables or dog kennels.*
Some shy youngsters have a great gift with animals, and this does bring them into contact with people of similar interests.

● *Let them join a political party, or CND, or Keep The Footpaths Open, or some other organisation.*
They'll meet people of all types, not be required to say much unless they want to, and feel that they have something in common with the others.

● *Praise shy teenagers, make them feel good.*
This love that you show will give them the confidence, the safe base, to face the busy, hustling world we live in. If your youngster is shy, deal with its disadvantages but don't try to change him or her. Shyness can be, and often is, very attractive, so why be ashamed of being shy? Most of us are, but few of us would ever admit it.

● *Make shy youngsters feel accepted, loved and respected as people.*
This gives them self-respect and provides an overcoat

that they can wear when life's winds blow strongly. People are born shy, but shyness need not be a handicap. What you need to know, when you're shy, is that you belong somewhere and that there is someone who loves you for who you are. This gives you self-respect and, shy or not, a real, unshakeable confidence.

A last word about shyness. If you as a parent are shy, and feel rather isolated in the home, you could set a good example by taking that first step yourself and finding a part-time job, or joining an evening class, or doing some voluntary work (your local Citizens' Advice Bureau will tell you which local organisations need volunteers). Many, many people are shy (including, oddly enough, some famous actors and actresses). It takes courage to take that first step, but the rewards in terms of companionship and making new friends are worth it.

MORE ABOUT SEX AND LOVE

I want to turn now to other problems about which parents of teenagers frequently seek my advice. Let's start off with problems of love and relating to the opposite sex. You'll want to prevent your youngsters from being hurt, so let's see what you can do and what you can't. All parents have to draw the line between too much freedom and overprotection. It isn't easy to get that line exactly right all the time. You'll make mistakes. We all do. What counts is your general manner or style of approach.

Laura, a 14-year-old girl, has made a friend of Mark, who is 16. Mark doesn't have a job and waits each afternoon to meet Laura coming out of school. Laura's school work has deteriorated over the six months that she's known Mark. Laura's mother is very worried about it. She decides to tackle Laura about the situation.

There are two ways Laura's mother can go about this. She can opt for confrontation or negotiation. She can say something like: 'I've had enough of your seeing that Mark. You're going to stop seeing him, d'you hear? You'll end up on the dole like him. You're going to come home straight from school and do your homework. I'm going to tell your father about this and your teachers. I'm fed up with you. You're going to give up that Mark and do what I say for a change. He's a lazy good-for-nothing and he's leading you into bad ways. You'll end up in trouble, you see if you don't.'

This approach helps mother to express her anger and annoyance, it helps her to get her feelings out into the open. It does nothing to solve the situation, however. Mother's words contain orders, threats, warnings, dire predictions. They make Laura feel belittled, devalued, angry, resentful. Mother's words are *damaging*. They damage the relationship and mar the possibility of a worked-out, mutual solution to the problem.

Take another way of handling this problem. Mother says something like: 'Laura, you know what a worrier I am? Well, I'm worried about your school work. Can we have a talk about it sometime? What about Thursday evening, before you go to bed? We can have a good chat and see if we can sort something out between us.' The words are dignified, and Laura is treated as a responsible person. Mother says it's a problem for her: she also indicates that the problem has a solution if the two of them decide, together, on the best thing to do.

In the talk on the Thursday evening, mother avoids interrogation. She simply says: 'Tell me how you feel about Mark.' Then she listens. She asks: 'What do you feel about your school work?' and 'What do you think has been happening at school?' She listens. Then she asks: 'How important is school to you?' Then, mother says something like: 'It isn't easy when you're young. You must feel there's a lot of pressure on you. All that school work and wanting to be with Mark.' This reflects back something of what Laura feels about her situation.

After an unhurried talk, in which mother does most of the listening, mother asks: 'What do you think is the best thing you can do to solve it?' This gives Laura the responsibility. It also implies that mother trusts Laura sufficiently to work out a solution that works for her.

Laura agrees to see Mark one evening a week and at

weekends. She laughs, 'I've been seeing too much of him, anyway.'

'I'll stop worrying,' says mother. 'You know how I worry,' adds mother. She laughs. So does Laura.

It's openness and honesty, shared feelings and mutual respect which solve problems. A parent has to show consideration for how the teenager feels and be honest about his or her own feelings. This enables the teenager to feel safe and trusted. It's style that counts. The style has to be calm and sensible. It's a discussion, not an argument. There isn't a winner and a loser. At the end of the discussion, both sides still have their dignity and respect each other more for having been open and honest with each other.

Many parents find it alarming that some girls of school age sleep with their boyfriends. I find it very worrying. What I want to know is how many of these girls can cope *emotionally* with a sexual relationship? I'd also like to know why the girl behaves in this way. Is there peer pressure on her not to be a virgin? Has her boyfriend talked her into it without any real consideration of her wishes and needs? Has the girl a good self-regarding sentiment, and does she realise that she has the right to say no? 'No' is always an option where there's real choice.

If you as a parent suspect that your under-age daughter is sleeping with her boyfriend, what can you do about it? You can't force her by threats, lectures, punishments, sanctions or insults to stop seeing the boy. How would you enforce that? Lock her in her bedroom? Every single day? What you have to do is to discuss it, in a way that both you and your teenager can hold on to your dignity and self-esteem.

It won't be easy. You may feel angry, shocked, alarmed. However, you're going to have to take a mature look at the situation, and what you'll want to know first is the answer to the practical problem of whether your daughter is taking precautions against becoming pregnant. It's information you want, and all the angry words and threats in the world won't help you to negotiate a solution.

How do you go about the problem? You don't condone the relationship, or give a moral lecture. You have a talk to your daughter about contraception. You say what you think and feel about bringing an unwanted baby into the world, about abortion, about how we have to act responsibly if we are to give all children who are born a chance to lead a happy life. This conversation can take place in the kitchen, over a cup of coffee, or whilst you're out shopping. Let your daughter have her say, too.

You then say something like: 'It's not for me to violate your privacy, but there's something I want you to do for me.' You then ask her to make an appointment to see the family doctor so that she can discuss with him or her the question of contraceptive measures. Make sure she does it, and keeps the appointment. When you have done that, you can talk about love, the morality of the relationship, the wisdom of having sexual relationships at such a young age, but only when you have taken steps to ensure that your daughter is not at risk concerning pregnancy.

After this has been done you can treat her as a mature, sensible person or as a sinner, an outcast. You can chat about love, about when you were young, about how things are different now. You can ask her: 'How are things going with John?' This brings it out into the open. It gives her a chance to continue the relationship, or perhaps decide that sex is putting too much pressure on it and end it. She has to decide for herself.

If you make her feel guilty, dirty and rejected she'll move further and further away from you and lose your support just when she needs it most. It's those non-judgemental talks, the knowledge that she can talk to you if she wants to, that give her a chance to keep her self-respect and not resort to secretive, furtive patterns of behaviour which may seriously damage the parent–teenager relationship.

Teenagers don't want to talk to parents about everything. They want to keep some aspects of their lives private. It's those parents who send out signals reading, 'Talk to me about it if you want to, and I shan't put you down if you do,' that teenagers feel safest with.

Take love. Every teenager who falls in love thinks he or she is the only person it's ever happened to. That doesn't mean you belittle that love. It's love and relationships which are the major cause of stress with teenagers. Young love can be marvellous; it can also drive young people to despair, to drugs, to alcohol, to suicide. That's why we must never, ever, take it less than seriously.

If you have a teenager in love you can say something like, 'Love is wonderful. It can also be very painful.' Say it with your arm around his or her shoulder. Say something about your own experiences of the agony and the ecstasy, the pain and the pleasure of love. You know what it feels like. What you have to get across, by a brief word or a talk over a cup of tea, is that you know what it feels like. Perhaps you can't help the course of young love to run smooth, but you can show you sympathise.

Just say, 'Tell me about it' (if your youngster looks sad). Or say, 'Talk to me about it if you want to.' Don't push it, it's a delicate business. Teenagers live in a tough, increasingly competitive world. The only thing that hasn't changed down through the centuries is young love. It's always been problematic, and it needs sensitive handling as far as parents are concerned.

Don't pick up your daughter's or son's mood. Don't you go mooning around the house as though you've lost something. You can be brisk and robust but still reflect back the teenager's feelings. 'You're in love,' you could say. 'You feel different.' Then you could add, 'I'm glad I'm not in love. You can't concentrate on things when you're in love. You keep thinking about the other person.'

Leave it at that. You'll think of your own things to say to convey your sympathy. No put-downs, no jokes (love isn't a joke). No disparaging remarks and no prying. You can, if you wish (and if you can be sincere, with just a dash of humour), talk to your teenager about your first love. It will, if done with sympathy, show how we all go through this tremendous experience with all its pleasure, confusion and intensity (most of us remember the first love of our lives).

I want to talk about other matters now and mention, again, the importance of being open and honest within the family. On some things you'll have strong opinions. That's fine. It's the way you put your views across that counts. On some things you'll want to make your own judgement. That's OK, but remember that your teenager is entitled to make a judgement too. It isn't a trial with you as judge and your teenager in the dock. It's open, honest negotiation. That's the best road to everybody agreeing to agree or disagree. What we're after is decisions taken on the basis of valid information and open discussion.

SMOKING

Take cigarettes. What you *could* do is to say something like, 'Don't ever let me catch you smoking.' If you think about it, that's almost a challenge. The parent isn't saying, 'Don't smoke.' He or she implies that the teenager wants to smoke and the name of the game is not to be caught doing it.

Let's take another approach. You're sitting at the tea-table, or just washing up the dishes in the kitchen with one of your teenagers. If you smoke yourself you could say, 'I wish I didn't smoke' (if you do wish that). If you don't smoke say, 'I'm glad I don't smoke' (if you are). It's what comes next that's important.

'Have you ever thought' you say, 'that smoking 20 cigarettes a day costs around £10 a week? That's £520 a year. You could buy a second-hand car or go on holiday for that. Smoking is certainly an expensive habit.' That's true. You're stating facts. There's no bombast, no over-heavy moral tone. You can't force your teenagers to accept your views; you can have a democratic discussion about real issues.

Then you can talk about the health risks: the shortness of breath, bronchitis, lung cancer. There's no way you can prevent teenagers experimenting with cigarette smoking if they want to. You *can* say (and this is your judgement): 'Anyone who smokes is a mug really. It's money down the drain and you lose your health into the bargain.' Say it quietly, don't overdo it. They'll make up their own minds, and the more they know that you trust them to decide wisely, the more likely they are to choose well.

It's the same with marijuana and other drugs. Drugs are widely available within the teenage culture. What you want is for your own youngster to say 'no', quietly and firmly. That's why it's OK to say, 'I don't know much about drugs, but they scare me. They can ruin a young person's life, have him or her turn to crime to get the money to pay for drugs, convert a healthy young person into a physical and mental wreck.' That's true. You're entitled to say it. It's the way you say it that counts. That way has to be sincere and in the context of an open discussion.

The truth is that many youngsters will experiment with marijuana, just as they'll smoke a cigarette or drink at the pub. They'll do these things because they *are* forbidden. It's the way parents react (and forbid) that's important. If you find a marijuana cigarette in the pocket of your daughter's coat, you might say: 'This is a bit stupid, isn't it?' and leave it at that. What will make her carry on with the forbidden behaviour are threats, warnings of dire punishment and abuse. 'If ever I catch you smoking one of these again . . .' *doesn't* work. She'll simply make sure you don't catch her.

HEALTHY LIVING

A father I know once said to his 16-year-old daughter: 'I don't mind you going down to the pub. If you make sure you get enough sleep and look after your health, that's fine with me.' The girl, who'd been drinking four or five nights a week with friends, started going at weekends only. Father had put the responsibility for her behaviour on her. He'd taken the 'forbidden' sign down and just pointed out, calmly, *one* disadvantage of going to the pub quite so often. When parents talk to teenagers, attitude is everything.

Compare that with another father who, when he found his daughter had been to a pub drinking with friends, said to her: 'You teenagers today are all drug addicts, sex maniacs and drunkards, and the whole stinking lot of you can go to hell as far as I'm concerned.' That's expressing feelings all right, but the net result, since there's no negotiation and a great deal of disparagement, is to make the daughter *more* rebellious. The daughter will drink even more, and the father will think, 'I'm right about teenagers.' He isn't. There's been no negotiation, no conciliation. The daughter is being invited to try more and better ways of upsetting her parents, to eat more forbidden fruits.

What we're after is a style of parenting that sets some boundaries (teenagers need these so that they can have something to rebel against), but places the responsibility for acting sensibly more and more in the hands of the teenager as he or she grows older. We as parents are entitled to express an opinion and to give the facts. Make sure that they are the facts, that they're relevant, and that the interpretation of them (i.e. your opinion) is expressed in a sincere, sensible way.

There will be problems you'll be able to deal with yourself. If you catch your son reading a 'soft porn' (or 'hard porn') magazine say, as a dad: 'I used to read those at your age. They degrade women.' As a mother you could say. 'You get a curious view of women in those mags, don't you? Women are real people, you know.' That's all that's needed. If he wants to read those kinds of mags, he will. If you forbid him to read them he'll merely hide them from you, and in addition feel guilty about his own feelings and sexuality.

There'll be other problems when your teenager talking to a neutral person, or to the family doctor, will be better than you trying to tackle the problem yourself. Teenage girls have worries about their bodies, about menstruation, about why one breast is bigger than the other, or about why their breasts are so big or so small. They worry about their skin, their complexions, about why their periods are so heavy or haven't started yet.

Do encourage your daughter to make an appointment to see the family doctor to talk about her worries. Take her up to the surgery, but let her talk to the doctor in private. A few words of reassurance can save months of worry, and those words of reassurance need to come from someone who has the authority and the empathy to allay the fears of the teenager concerned.

You must tell your teenage son that if he is at any time worried about spots, rashes or blemishes on any part of his body, or about the size of his penis or any other worry that he has regarding his health, he must similarly see the family doctor. GPs are used to dealing with these problems and can often help a troubled teenager get a particular worry sorted out.

If you have doubts about your daughter's eating habits and feel she isn't eating enough (and losing too much weight), do consult your doctor. Teenage girls often want to slim, but where losing weight becomes obsessive and secretive, then there is a chance of anorexia nervosa ('the slimmers' disease') taking hold, and this nervous lack of appetite can be very serious. Some girls tell their parents of the food they've eaten during the day when in reality they've eaten nothing, and others begin to really believe that they're overweight when in fact they are thin and undernourished. The solution is: if in doubt, see your doctor.

The signs to look out for are an obsessive interest in body weight and a marked anxiety about eating, even when very hungry. There may be marked weight loss, together with abnormal menstrual periods or loss of menstrual periods. The teenage girl (only 4 per cent of anorexics are male) will insist that she is fat, overweight and unattractive when she is still attractive, though dangerously thin. Do get help with this problem *before* it becomes a chronic illness.

As associated condition is bulimia nervosa. Here the teenager overeats, goes on a binge (usually of carbohydrate foods), and then makes herself vomit after the binge. Bulimics often eat a staggering amount of food during a binge and then, to relieve their physical and mental discomfort, their feelings of self-disgust and revulsion, deliberately make themselves sick.

Again there is an avid preoccupation with body weight and a loss of control over eating habits. There is a preoccupation with food preparation. The girl may have marked fluctuations in weight, irregular periods, bad teeth (the acids from the stomach affect the teeth) together with bad breath. There may be bloating of the abdomen and an irregular, racing heartbeat (tachycardia). There may be over-secretiveness, periods of depression together with bursts of anger and hostility directed towards other people. Girls with bulimia nervosa can, however, be very outgoing and socially popular.

They become skilled at hiding the fact that they suffer from this disorder.

With marked weight increase or weight loss in girls, the safest thing is to consult your family doctor. Most teenage girls are interested in their weight and their figures. It is when this interest becomes totally obsessive, to the detriment of their general health, that parents need to seek advice.

For a long time now I have been involved in sorting out people's personal problems: first, as a psychologist working with families in a clinic setting and second, as agony uncle with *Cosmopolitan* magazine. One thing I've learned: you don't solve people's problems for them. You help them to solve those problems themselves. What you do is give people reassurance, encouragement. You tell them what choices they have, what decisions they *can* make, if they want to, to solve the problem.

You give them information if they need it. You give them the facts, tell them what help is available to them and how to set about getting that help. You respect them as individuals, as they are, and hope that the changes that they make will bring them the happiness they seek. You shouldn't criticise them, preach at them, judge them. You *should* act as a friend and give practical help.

It's exactly the same with parents and their teenagers. We can give them the facts, sketch in the choices they have, say what we see to be a possible solution. Then, it's up to them. More than our answers, they seek our reassurance and our encouragement. They'll cope, but they'll cope a lot better if they know that they can come to us, talk openly and honestly, and be listened to, not lectured at.

To help teenagers with their personal problems, you must learn to:

- *Get along with them.*
  Talk to them as you would talk to a good adult friend. If you have an opinion, state your case but state it without resorting to bitterness, diatribes or insults.

- *A very useful sentence with teenagers is: 'Tell me about it.'*
  Don't forget to listen if they choose to.

- *Don't expect them to talk to you about everything.*
  There'll be things your teenagers will choose to keep to themselves. That's fine. Just make it clear that you don't want to know everything but that they can talk to you if they want to.

- *They may not want to talk to you about sex.*
  That's OK. It's their choice. Remember, you tell them quite a lot about your attitude to sex, and other things too, in your general attitudes and behaviour, not to mention off-the-cuff remarks. We don't have to discuss something with those we live close to in order to learn what they feel about it.

- *Your views may change.*
  Who cares? We all change our mind. Sometimes it's impossible to be consistent in our views. What we should aim to be consistent in is our ongoing respect for our teenagers and their views. Mutual respect and mutual problem-solving is more important than consistency.

- *Don't be secretive yourself.*
  Don't try to hide things from teenagers. Be open and honest about what you're thinking and feeling. That creates an atmosphere in which they can be open and honest too.

- *Expect problems.*
  You're an unusual parent indeed if you never have any problems. Talk to friends about them, don't hide them. If you still can't solve the problem, then get professional help. You're not Sigmund Freud, and sometimes it's essential to have a professional person's advice. It can save a great deal of time, pain and sorrow.

9
Growing up together

In this last section of the book I want to draw some conclusions about parents and teenagers. You, as a parent can offer practical help and genuine care and support to your teenager. What you ask in return is some consideration for you as a parent and as an adult who happens to live in the same house. Negotiation is always a two-way process: give and take.

What you can *give* to your teenager is affection. To know that one is loved is very important to all human beings, so do show your teenager affection. It may just be a word of tenderness, an arm around the shoulder, a hug, or the simple words, 'I do love you, you know,' (even if you do add, 'though you get on my nerves at times'). There's a taboo on tenderness in our society. I think it's sad. If you love your youngster, you have to show it.

You can also give your youngster some of your time. Time is a great thief. It steals our youth, it steals our children, then it steals our life away from us. It's no use, if you're a busy father or mother, saying: 'I'll spend some time with my teenagers next week or next year when I'm less busy.' Whilst you're saying that, your chances of establishing a genuine friendship and partnership with them are slipping away. Do get to know your teenagers while you still have time.

Do establish a style of parenting that is honest, open and reasonably cool. Don't blow your top one day and be affectionate the next, or have rules one day and forget about them the next. Establish what the rules are, then stick to them. Be consistent. Let your teenagers know what's expected of them, what they can and can't do. Say no when you need or want to, and don't forget you have rights as well as duties.

Accentuate the positive. Say things like: 'Put your clothes

away,' rather than 'Who's left this stuff all over the place?' If you give an order, mean it, stick to it. At the same time, always remember to praise your teenagers when they've achieved something, rather than always nagging them when they get on your nerves, or shouting at them when they behave badly. Behaviour which is rewarded tends to be repeated. Often we get bad behaviour from teenagers simply because it's only when teenagers behave badly that we pay them any attention.

Don't use threats, such as 'Do that again and there'll be real trouble.' Why say this sort of thing? It's better to say, 'I don't like that. Cut it out.' Say it sharply, briskly, and mean it. Teenagers aren't stupid. They'll get the picture. Elaborate threats, warnings and abuse are often quite useless in actually dealing with bad behaviour. They are, sometimes, a challenge to the youngster to behave even worse.

Don't blame yourself for everything that happens to your teenagers. They have rights as well. They have choices to make, and sometimes they'll make the wrong choices. There are other influences on their lives besides parents. All you can do is to love them beyond reason, try to give them practical help if and when they do run into trouble, and try to provide a safe base (the family) to which they can return having lost, won, been hurt or been triumphant as the case may be. You can't live their lives for them; they have to learn to live their own lives.

What parents tend to forget is that they send out hidden, unconscious messages to their youngsters. It's the tone of the conversation, and the attitude behind the words actually said, that affect youngsters. In some families the unspoken family motto is: 'This will all end in tears.' The daily conversation in the home is depressing, discouraging, pessimistic. The parents, anxious about money or the state of the world, persistently convey their own anxieties and insecurities to their teenagers. Our general attitude to the world has a deep effect on our youngsters.

Consider Family A. They constantly discuss divorce, the deterioration of the world since 1960, the terrible crimes reported on TV or in the newspapers, and the awful economic plight of the country together with their own economic plight. These discussions or comments are accompanied by gloomy prognostications regarding the future of the world. The message is: 'The world is getting worse and we find it all very depressing, difficult to cope with, rather hopeless.' Teenagers, though, must learn to cope, must learn not to be too depressed, must live with hope.

Family B, in contrast, are hard up, but they *do things* . They save up and go on an inexpensive camping holiday every summer. They've managed to buy a frame tent for £50. The parents go camping together and each or all of their three teenagers can go with them if they wish. Mother says: 'We live cheaply. It costs no more than staying at home.' Mother has a part-time job. Father doesn't earn a great deal, but they both go to a judo club which they attend once a week. They always have some plan, some project on the go. The message, unspoken, is: 'The world is what you make it. We don't have much money but we're getting as much fun and enjoyment out of our lives as we possibly can.'

These unspoken, hidden messages within families are extremely important. There *are* many terrible things – terrorism, murder, rape – that happen in the world, but there are also many marvellous people in the world, people who are generous kind, honest. When you talk to your teenagers, you have to get across the message that there is good in the world as well as evil, hope as well as despair, a chance to do something to improve the quality of life as well as just sit there and say, 'Life's awful.' Teenagers *are* affected by parents' attitude to the world, so do stress the good things that go on as well as the bad. That gives a more balanced picture of the world. It avoids an all-pervading despondency which depresses or alarms youngsters, who are interested in making the world a better place.

You may or may not be a hero to your teenager, but at least you can be honest and open to him or her. If you're asked a question and you don't know the answer, say so and if you can, suggest where he or she could find out. If you're asked for your opinion, give it. You have a right to an opinion. The opinion's less important than the attitude behind it. You should be serious and absolutely honest in your answer; no bombast, no insisting that you're the only one who knows. The teenager will make up his or her mind anyway. What you can do is show that we are, all of us, entitled to put our point of view and we have a duty to listen to the points of view of others. It's the style and the manner of answering which are more important than the answer itself. A hero you may not be, but at least your youngster will know that he or she can rely on you for an honest answer, or you can find an answer together. That, in my view, is more useful than being a hero to him or her. It means you're real and you can work things out together, rather than blindly following only one point of view.

With teenagers, you do have to try to live your own life rather than being too involved with their lives. It's their spring, not yours, but it can be your Indian summer. When my own mother was 40 she had lost her figure, was worn out with bringing up her four children and, if truth be told, had little to look forward to other than seeing her children achieve the goals they had set themselves. My mother was a 'mum'. If you'd suggested to her that she was a person as well, she would have been puzzled. Her primary role in life was the rearing of her children.

Nowadays it isn't like that. Mothers and fathers are people as well as parents. So do keep growing and developing as a person alongside your children. They'd rather relate to a viable, energetic human being than to someone who says things like: 'I'm just a mum,' or 'being a dad has worn me out.' I don't mean that you should imitate your teenagers, ape them, try to be like them. That would be silly. I do mean that you have plenty of your own life left and that you should have some goals and ambitions of your own, you should be a person in your own right. This will make it easier, not harder, for you to allow your teenagers to be the same.

The main thing to remember about teenagers is that they are not a sub-species of human beings, they *are* human beings. They're not morons, ETs or always undergoing emotional crises. They are often less sophisticated, more emotionally vulnerable than they look, but that doesn't mean that they are morons or incapable of understanding practical necessities and moral issues. It is the way those necessities and issues are presented to them which will determine their response. I think the best way to present them is for us adults and parents to ask: 'What shall we do about this *together?*'

It has to be remembered that there's a great deal of difference between a 13-year-old and an 18-year-old. We have to release the reins of control gradually so that teenagers may learn to take responsibility for themselves, learn to make their own choices. Princess Di was a teenager when Prince Charles proposed to her. Teenagers is an umbrella term, but there are all sorts of teenagers and we have to take into account, when we're dealing with them, who they are, their age, stage of development and emotional maturity. Why make generalisations about teenagers when each one of them is different and a person in his or her own right?

It can be a difficult age, and that's why teenagers do sometimes opt for a secret language, a teenage culture, a private land to which no adult owns a passport. That's fair enough. We don't want to be intruders in that land. At the same time, there's a great deal of sameness as well as difference when it comes to teenagers and adults. So don't exaggerate the differences, don't patronise and don't treat them as though they were creatures form outer space. Many of them are lively, energetic, incredibly mature and sensible, so give credit where credit is due and treat them with the respect and admiration that many of them deserve.

Some people believe that parenting is a dead-end job. No sooner have you learned to do it well than you become redundant. I don't believe that. I think what you teach your youngsters they carry around with them for the rest of your lives. If you teach them love, they'll know you're always there when they need you. You are the safe base from which they go out to explore the world. Parents are never redundant.

You must not only love your children, you must protect them. The best way to do that is to make them 'street-wise', teach them how to cope. You have to learn not to be possessive, over-protective. They must survive in the rough seas of life, so you can't say: 'Don't go near the water.' You must teach them how to swim, encourage them to develop skills of their own and, at an appropriate age and stage do things and go places on their own. That's the only way to teach them how to survive in the world.

Your love mustn't be selfless. It must take your needs and wishes into account. The danger with totally selfless love is that it turns into martyrdom or resentment. Be selfish from time to time or, at least, don't forget to be kind to yourself as well as them. Nobody wants totally selfish parents, and no youngster wants parents to say: 'You do that, and after all I've done for you.' Help your child to make decisions that are best for everyone, because everyone in the family has needs. Families that work take everyone's needs into account, not just the needs of those who are the most vociferous, demanding or manipulating. Be a self-respecting parent rather than selfish or selfless.

Parents are often given advice on how they can change their children's behaviour. Less often are parents advised to change themselves. That's a difficult thing to do.

Think about it. In your job you may have to change your role. In your adult friendships roles may change, with you sometimes being the strong, supportive one and sometimes being the one who's in need of a shoulder to cry on. It's the same in your relationship with your spouse. That relationship should change, grow, develop. So should your relationship with your youngsters, and that doesn't mean that it's they who do all the adjustment.

The family is an organic, not a static, entity. It changes and grows over the years. The nature of parental authority changes from being fairly autocratic ('Because I say so') to being more open, democratic ('These are my reasons. Tell me what you think and I'll promise to listen'). When you as a parent have a problem, share it, be open, and this will teach your youngsters to be open and honest about their problems. If you have a disagreement, aim for the best possible solution and stick to it. Nobody wins, nobody loses. Families are about power, and the use of power, as well as love. The way to handle power is to share it, discuss it, allocate responsibility and give everybody a feeling that you're not keeping all the power to yourself. That's autocracy, not democracy, and autocracy leads to rebellion and a rejection of the values that you are trying, too forcibly, to instil.

If things are going wrong in your family, it may be because you're being too rigid, too critical, too watchful. You may want to control and direct your teenagers too much, to limit and restrict them or worse try to make them live out your fantasies or achieve where you failed. That's not fair. They have their own fantasies to live out, they have their own dreams, and those are what we must hope come true for them.

So step back a little. Let them be. Don't try to control every aspect of their lives. If your methods of dealing with your teenagers don't work, change them. If your attitudes provoke aggression and unco-operation, be prepared to look at those attitudes and accept the possibility that it's *you* who may be wrong. This is hard to accept, I know, but all I'm saying is that you may be expecting too much from them: expecting them to be what you want them to be rather than encouraging them to become the best possible people they can be. Don't fuss, nag, worry all the time. Let it go and have faith in them. What will be, will be – whether you worry or not. So don't worry about them too much and don't be too censurious of them. They're not like you. They are themselves.

Treat your children with respect and they will treat you with respect in return. Don't try to mould them to some preconceived pattern, and don't try to make them into replicas of yourself. They are human beings in their own right. You don't own them. They are merely on loan to you and you must teach them something good and honest and true while they are passing through your hands. Kahlil Gibran, in his book *The Prophet* (Heinemann), has, in my view, the right attitude towards the relationship of children and parents. He tells parents something very profound. Gibran says that we *don't* own our children: they are simply on loan to us. We cannot possess them; we can only guide them and give them love. Here is what Gibran had to say:

Your children are not your children.
They are the sons and daughters of Life's
longing for itself.
They come through you but not from you,
And though they are with you yet they belong
not to you.
You may give them your love but not your
thoughts,
For they have their own thoughts.
You may house their bodies but not their souls,
For their souls dwell in the house of tomorrow,
which you cannot visit, not even in your dreams.
You may strive to be like them,
but seek not to make them like you.
For life goes not backwards nor tarries with
yesterday.
You are the bows from which your children as
living arrows are sent forth.

These words were written more than 60 years ago, but they are just as relevant now as they were then. We must love our children, but we must give them separateness and space to live their own lives; for they are the children of tomorrow and we, as parents, must respect that tomorrow will not be the same as yesterday or today. That is why we must learn to listen to them and not be too rigid in our own attitudes, too possessive with them. It is they, not us, who possess the future.

We are rushing at a tremendous pace towards the twenty-first century. We are all living in a time of constant change, new ideas, new ways of living, new attitudes to what life is about. Some people believe that our society is morally bankrupt. I don't. I find many people moral, caring, kind, aware of those less well off than themselves, concerned about the poverty of the Third World and concerned about the poor and underprivileged in our own society. I find that caring, concern and sensitivity especially prevalent amongst the young.

As we move rapidly towards a brand-new century, we will

learn that people cannot live by bread alone. Unless we are to enter a spiritual Dark Ages, my guess is that the psychology of the future will be Adlerian rather than Freudian, with an emphasis on the group rather than individuals, with an emphasis on *Gemeinschaftgefuhl* (community feeling) rather than selfishness, with a movement towards seeing the earth on which we live as one world, rather than a collection of self-seeking and selfish nations. The keyword of the future is We, not I, as we strive to live in a family, in a country, or on this planet, together.

So do teach your youngsters some ideals. Don't be cynical, pessimistic. Human beings of any age need hope and ideals. They need to believe that *everybody* is of worth, no matter what their race, colour or creed may be. If we are to survive we must lose our prejudices, get to know each other and learn to live in harmony and honest give-and-take, whether we be parent and teenager, black and white, Protestant and Catholic, rich or poor, and whether we live in East or West or the Third World. We must learn to live together, in peace, in the global village which the world now is. That's the vital lesson to be learned before the new millennium.

That's why I've advocated an open and honest style of parenting in this book. It's a style in which you can state your case, say what your views are, argue things out (friends do argue sometimes), and work things out together. If teenagers want and get their own way all the time, the family won't work. If you insist on getting your own way all the time it won't work either. What you have to have is negotiation. What you have to remember is that you're a parent but it doesn't mean you're always right.

What makes a family work? I think it's getting the simple things right. I think it's treating your teenager as you'd treat a good friend, as someone who is a real person whom you like and respect. It's showing how pleased you are when your youngster has succeeded at something; it's not going on and on when they've failed. Encouragement works better than criticism. It's expressing your love simply (ruffling his hair, putting your arms around her), and saying: 'You're great. I Love you.' Everybody needs to know that. It's letting your children live their lives, not fussing too much but giving practical help and encouragement when it's needed. It's having faith in them, and in yourself.

What's needed is common sense, not complicated psychology. What's needed is a bit of space for everybody, so that each member of the group can gain support from the other without parents fulfilling their own dreams and fantasies through their children. Our children have to paint their own picture of the world, and it is the love and affection we show them, and the practical help, which give them a chance to get that picture right.

Here are Ten Rules for Parents to enable you to live your life and to help your teenagers to live theirs:

- *Accept yourself.*
  Accept that you have faults, that you're not perfect, that you don't always behave as others would want you to behave. This will help you to accept your teenagers, and their peculiarities.

- *Be a person as well as a mum or dad.*
  Have your own goals, aims, ambitions, dreams. Don't seek all your gratification from your children. Live alongside them, not through them. Don't use your children to give you a feeling of pride, self-respect and love. You can get those things elsewhere, and if you're too dependent on your children for your self-esteem, it will make you over-anxious and over-protective towards them. Love 'em and leave 'em be. You and they are destined to follow different roads in life, but you can share part of that road together and be good companions.

- *Try to believe that your teenagers want to be good.*
  Much of their happiness depends on parental approval, so don't overreact when things go wrong. Say: 'We'll do it better next time. We learn nothing from our successes. We should learn from our failures.' That gives them a chance to co-operate and be accepted.

●   *When you have to say no, stick to it.*
    It isn't love to say yes all of the time. That's fear, and it
    should play no part in good parenting or good friendship.

●   *Mean what you say and say what you mean.*
    You have a right to your views, but don't be rigidly
    authoritarian. Accept that the world is changing and that
    simple solutions to the problems which face us aren't
    always possible. Say what you have to say to your
    teenagers, but don't forget some of the time to listen to
    them.

●   *Don't underestimate your teenagers.*
    Don't be over-conscientious, over-protective, forever
    worrying about them. Have faith in them. They'll
    probably cope with their problems much better if you
    forget about them for a while, join an evening class and
    start worrying about *you*.

●   *Don't pass on hand-me-down values to your teenagers.*
    What worked for your parents with you may not work
    with them. Why not work it out together? Then you both
    learn something and you stop making your teenagers fit
    into a preconceived mould.

●   *Respect your teenagers.*
    They are human beings with real feelings and emotions.
    Respect those feelings. Treat your teenagers with the
    same kind of respect that you show to your adult friends.
    You don't treat your friends as ETs so why should you
    treat teenagers that way?

●   *Tell them the truth, as you see it.*
    Don't try to hide the truth. It's what they don't know that
    frightens children of all ages, not what they know. They
    live in a dangerous, changing world and they have to be
    'street-wise' and adaptable. They'll never be that if we try
    to run away from unpalatable facts. Tell them how you
    feel, what's worrying you, and what makes you happy.

Talk about feelings and emotions, about what's going on inside you. That will make them feel safer. If you never tell them the truth about you, how can they get to know you as a person?

- *Teenagers are just as important as babies and young children.*
  They may sometimes be more difficult to deal with. If you run into trouble and can't handle it yourself, do try to find help. Sometimes, when we share a problem with other parents or with an expert counsellor, what we had seen as an insurmountable difficulty becomes a problem that can be solved. (Useful addresses are given at the back of the book.)

My own three erstwhile teenagers are grown up now. They no longer live in the family house. One lives in London, another in Switzerland, the youngest in York. The house is very quiet without them. You may believe it's absolutely awful with teenagers about the place. Believe me, it's terribly dull when they've gone. So don't forget to have fun with them some of the time, and talk to them. They're quite interesting, really. What's surprising is how they turn into sensible, friendly adults. Whether that's because of Mother Nature, or our efforts as parents when they go through that teenage stage, I don't know. I suspect that Kahlil Gibran is right. You are the bow, they are the arrows, and the bow has to take some of the strain. The reward is to see the arrows fly through the air, independent, free, heading towards the target of self-fulfilment.

Useful addresses

CAREERS

Careers Service
9 Carmelite Street
LONDON
EC4Y 0JE

(01) 353 1595

The number of your local
Careers Service will be in the
phone book.

DRUGS

Aid for Addicts and Family
(ADFAM)
82 Old Brompton Road
London
SW7 3LQ

(01) 823 9313

There are local groups. Ask at
your Citizens' Advice Bureau.

Drug Advisory Centre
9A Brockley Cross
LONDON
SE4 2AB

(01) 692 4975

The address of your local
Centre will be in the phone
book.

Release
169 Commercial Street
LONDON
E1 6BW

(01) 377 5905

Ring (01) 603 8654 if it is an
emergency.

Alcohol

Al-Anon Family Groups
61 Great Dover Street
LONDON
SE1 4YF

(01) 403 0888

Alcoholics Anonymous
P O Box 1
Stonebow House
Stonebow
YORK
YO1 2NJ

(0904) 644026

Glue sniffing

Kick It
13 Tarbert Close
Bletchley
MILTON KEYNES
MK2 3EY

(0908) 368869

EDUCATION

Advisory Centre for Education
(ACE)
18 Victoria Park Square
LONDON
E2 9PB

(01) 980 4597

Dyslexia Institute
133 Gresham Road
STAINES
Middlesex
TW18 2AJ

(0784) 459498

Education Otherwise
Heathermead
25 Common Lane
HEMMINGFORD ABBOTS
Cambridgeshire

(0480) 63130

Exists to help parents who
wish to educate their children
at home.

FAMILY

Gingerbread
35 Wellington Street
LONDON
WC2E 7BN

(01) 240 0953

For one-parent families.

National Marriage Guidance
Council
Herbert Gray College
Little Church Street
RUGBY
Warwickshire
CV21 3AP

(0788) 73241

Help for parents and teenagers
on family problems and sexual
relationships.

HEALTH

Health Education Authority
Hamilton House
Mabledon Place
London
WC1

(01) 631 0930

Scottish Health Education
Group
Health Education Centre
Woodburn House
Canaan Lane
EDINBURGH
EH10 4SG

(031) 447 8044

Both will provide useful
leaflets on how to become fit
and healthy and how to stay
that way.

Anorexia nervosa

Anorexic Aid
The Priory Centre
11 Priory Road
HIGH WYCOMBE
Buckinghamshire

(0494) 21431

LAW

Citizens' Advice Bureaux
326 St Pauls Road
Islington
LONDON
N1

(01) 359 0619

The CAB have local offices (the address will be in your phone book), and can provide free and confidential information on any subject.

National Council for Civil Liberties
21 Tabard Street
LONDON
SE1 4LA

(01) 403 3888

LEISURE

National Association of Young People's Counselling Services (NAYPCAS)
17–23 Albion Street
LEICESTER
LE1 6GD

(0533) 558763

The Sports Council
16 Upper Woburn Place
LONDON
WC1H OQP

(01) 388 1277

Scottish Sports Council
Caledonia House
South Dyle
EDINBURGH
EH12 9DQ

(031) 317 7200

Youth Hostels Association
Trevelyan House
ST ALBANS
Hertfordshire
AL1 2DX

SEX

British Pregnancy Advisory Service
Austy Manor
Wootton Wawen
SOLIHULL
West Midlands
B95 6BX

Brook Advisory Centres
153A East Street
LONDON
SE17 2SD

(01) 708 1234 and 708 1390

Family Planning Association
27 Mortimer Street
LONDON
W1N 7RJ

(01) 636 7866

Gay Switchboard (London)

(01) 837 7324

For teenagers who are gay or who are not sure about it and wish to talk to someone.

SUICIDE

The Samaritans

Look up the number in your local telephone directory or ask the operator. In any crisis, but especially if somebody is deeply miserable and has mentioned killing themselves, the Samaritans are always available.

WELFARE RIGHTS

Ring your local Citizens' Advice Bureau. The number is in the telephone book.

Further Reading

How to Succeed at GCSE by John Bowden. Cassell 1989.
A useful book for teenagers and parents. It's very readable and deals with many of the difficulties teenagers have in working for GCSE.

Handwriting by Tom Gourdie MBE. Ladybird Books.
The modified italic style advocated in the book is easy to learn and 'tidies up' handwriting like a charm.

Cassell's Spelling Dictionary compiled by David Firnberg. Cassell 1985.

Logical Spelling by B. V. Allan. Collins 1977.
This makes clear some of the rules of spelling and emphasises the patterns of words which are similar.

The Essential Word Spelling List by Fred Schonell. Macmillan.
This inexpensive little book groups words into families so that the user is able to see the patterns of words, those which have the same beginnings or endings.

Drugs – What You Can Do as a Parent, issued by the Department of Health and Social Security and the Welsh Office.
This is a useful pamphlet which you can obtain from your local clinic or from the local reference library. It gives good, practical advice and is very easy to read.

The Unemployment Handbook by Guy Dauncey. National Extension College 1983.
This gives practical and detailed advice on jobhunting, together with clear explanations of unemployment benefit and supplementary benefit rights.